SISTER EMMANUEL

# The Forgotten Power of Fasting

*Healing, Liberation, Joy . . .*

© 2017 by Sr. Emmanuel Maillard.
All rights reserved.

Republished in 2020.
Book Design by Catholic Way Publishing.

Translated from Italian by Andrea and Elizabeth Bernazzoli.
Edited by Ann-Marie Chinnery and Christine Zaums.
Original Title: "Potenza sconosciuta del Digiuno"

Technical editor and graphic designer: Alessandro Agus, 2017.
Published by Children of Medjugorje, USA www.childrenofmedjugorje.com

The use of the expression: "Our Lady appeared" by the author does not mean that she had any intention of pre-empting the opinion of the Church authorities as to the authenticity of the apparitions of Mary in Medjugorje. The book contains only the personal opinion of the author, based on the testimony of those who have been witnesses to the events in the village. The purpose of publishing this book is to provide information to those who read it. Both author and publisher will submit their opinions to the discernment of the Church as soon as any formal pronouncement on these events is made.

Ordering Information:
Orders by trade bookstores and wholesalers.
Please contact Ingram Content at www.ingramcontent.com

ISBN-13: 978-0-9980218-7-4

11 10 9 8 7 6 5 4 3 2

Available in E-Book.

www.childrenofmedjugorje.com

# Contents

| | | |
|---|---|---:|
| Introduction | | 1 |
| 1. | Will You Jump? | 3 |
| 2. | Two Days out of Seven | 5 |
| 3. | Our Body | 14 |
| 4. | Prepare the Great Works of God | 18 |
| 5. | Protection | 20 |
| 6. | Purification from Evil | 23 |
| 7. | Fasting is Powerful | 25 |
| 8. | A Battlefield | 30 |
| 9. | Givers or Takers? | 32 |
| 10. | Facing Disastrous Paths, is There a Solution? | 34 |
| 11. | The Suggestions of Satan | 37 |
| 12. | Until the Completion of the Plan | 40 |
| 13. | Purgatory | 42 |
| 14. | Choosing to be Healed | 43 |
| 15. | Fasting for Children | 48 |
| 16. | Suspending the Laws of Nature | 51 |
| 17. | Satan Doesn't Give Gifts | 53 |
| 18. | Jesus Breaks Evil Bonds | 56 |
| Frequently Asked Questions | | 58 |
| | What kind of bread? | 58 |
| | What are the best times of day to fast? | 60 |

|   |   |
|---|---|
| What about those who are sick? | 61 |
| How much bread? | 63 |
| Why bread? | 66 |
| Why me? | 67 |
| Be the extended hands of God | 68 |
| See that you can do it? | 71 |
| Interview with Milona | 73 |
| Testimonials | 86 |
| "If I had known...!" | 86 |
| God defeats the insubordinate one | 88 |
| Patrick, freed from alcohol and gambling | 93 |
| Luca, a day of obedience | 95 |
| What the Saints Tell Us . . . | 100 |
| The shepherds of Fatima | 100 |
| St. John Paul II | 100 |
| Saint Faustina | 101 |
| Saint John Bosco: | 102 |
| Saint John Chrysostom | 105 |
| Saint Peter Chrysologus | 106 |
| Saint Alfonso Maria de Liguori | 107 |
| Saint Leo the Great | 107 |
| Saint Thomas Aquinas | 108 |
| Saint Augustine | 108 |
| Saint Cure of Ars | 108 |
| Saint Francis De Sales | 109 |
| Prayer for the night before fasting | 110 |
| Messages of Our Lady on Fasting | 112 |
| 1981 | 112 |
| 1982 | 113 |
| 1983 | 113 |
| 1984 | 114 |

| | |
|---|---:|
| 1985 | 116 |
| 1986 | 116 |
| 1987 | 117 |
| 1989 | 118 |
| 1991 | 119 |
| 1992 | 119 |
| 1999 | 121 |
| 2000 | 121 |
| 2001 | 122 |
| 2003 | 122 |
| 2004 | 123 |
| 2005 | 123 |
| 2006 | 124 |
| 2007 | 125 |
| 2008 | 127 |
| 2009 | 128 |
| 2010 | 128 |
| 2011 | 129 |
| 2012 | 130 |
| 2013 | 132 |
| 2014 | 136 |
| 2015 | 138 |
| Recipes | 139 |
|   Fasting Bread | 139 |
|   Another recipe for fasting bread | 140 |
|   Spelt Bread | 142 |
|   Marie-Line's recipe | 143 |
|   Sister Sarah's recipe for fasting bread | 145 |
|   Flavia's Recipe for Fasting bread Made without yeast like chapattis in India | 146 |
|   Instructions | 146 |
|   Gluten-Free Fasting Bread Recipe | 147 |

For a bread loaf of about 1.5 pounds (with dry fruits) in the bread machine. On cycle for wheat: 148

For a bread loaf of about 1lb (without dry fruits) in the bread machine. On cycle for Wheat or Integral: 149

Recipe for flat rye loaves 149

Recipe for English bread 150

Other Books from the Author 152

About the Author 163

*To those who are afraid to fast,*

*To all those who do not yet have the courage to fast,*

*To those who have started to fast,*

*To those who persevere in it*

*Also . . .*

*To those who have fasted for me*

*When I was in the darkness*

*Thanks to whom I could come to know the light*

## *Message of January 25, 2001*

"Dear Children! Today I call you to renew prayer and fasting with even greater enthusiasm until prayer becomes a joy for you. Little children, the one who prays is not afraid of the future and the one who fasts is not afraid of evil. Once again, I repeat to you: only through prayer and fasting also wars can be stopped, wars of your unbelief and fear for the future.

I am with you and am teaching you little children: your peace and hope are in God. That is why draw closer to God and put Him in the first place in your life. Thank you for having responded to my call."

# Introduction

When I started recording a CD about fasting, I knew it was my duty to do it, because fasting is an essential element in our journey with God. The whole Bible reveals it and the Queen of Peace strongly emphasizes it and recommends it as a weapon in the spiritual warfare of our times.

Still, I thought to myself that using the word "fasting" would prevent people from buying the CD. To console myself I said, "if only 50 people listen to the CD, for those 50 I would not have worked in vain!"

Then I turned the CD into a book, and it has not been like that at all! To my great surprise, it has quickly become a best-seller in French as well as in other languages! I received enthusiastic testimonies from people who had faithfully embraced fasting and obtained great benefits both spiritually and physically.

Strengthened by this encouragement and with the help of doctors and fervent souls, I decided to resume this writing (previously published). Thanks to a lot of research I have been able to enrich the original manuscript so as to respond to the needs of our times.

Throughout the book you will encounter Luca, Patrick and others... who will tell you how fasting has transformed their lives, obtaining for them graces of healing and liberation they never thought they could receive. You will enter into the deep sense of fasting. Far from seeing it as a penance to avoid, you will embrace it as an extraordinary instrument to receive freedom and peace in your heart. These are things you will not find on the overstocked shelves in our shopping centers.

This book offers you very practical advice on how to make the most of fasting and gives you the best recipes to bake your own fasting bread. You can share it with your loved ones and increase the number of "instruments of peace" so desired by the Lord.

Finally, the personal discovery of fasting will open a new dimension in your Christian life, will remove your fears and will make you a joyful disciple of Christ.

Enjoy reading…and start putting it into practice!

# 1. Will You Jump?

Let's start with a question to see if you are ready. Imagine walking along a river, it's December and it's freezing cold. All of a sudden you hear screams: it's a young boy drowning. The child is either two or three years old and if you don't help him, if you don't dive in to rescue him, he will die. What are you going to do? Dive in, knowing that the water is freezing cold? Really? Of course you would! You would want to save his life; you wouldn't let a child die when it is in your power to save him. It's so easy to dive in!

It is the same with fasting. Fasting gives us the opportunity to save many lives: it prevents young people from getting lost, children from dying, and families from separating. Unfortunately, for almost half a century in the western world, we have abandoned fasting and death has been able to bring unprecedented devastation. Have you noticed the coincidence between the abandonment of fasting and the invasion of the world by Satan and his demons? They have even easily infiltrated the Church, because its doors were no longer closed! In Medjugorje, the Queen of Peace launches an appeal, an anguished cry for our own good: "The west has abandoned fasting." We need to resume this practice. It is a very strong appeal!

Our Lady gives us five points to put into practice to become Saints, to have within us the fullness of love, and defeat Satan. These are fundamental steps in our journey toward God. However, the second one, fasting, is the one that many people don't want to consider.

Wherever I go in the world, even to the most remote parts, I meet people that have embraced the school of Medjugorje. I notice that they live four of the points very well: The Mass, reading the Bible, going to confession, and saying the rosary, but when I talk to them about fasting, they lower their heads and they don't answer... They have abandoned it. That's because we haven't understood what fasting really is! The Queen of Peace speaks about it in a very beautiful way and reveals its meaning as a powerful tool in our hands. God's power can accomplish, through us, the extraordinary things that we need.

## 2. Two Days out of Seven

Our Lady asks us to fast on bread and water two days a week, Wednesday and Friday. Why those two days? Our Lady, Saint Joseph, Jesus and all the Jews of those times, used to fast two days a week. Fasting is part of the Jewish and Christian religions, as well as Islam, Buddhism and Hinduism. Let's remember in a special way Gandhi and all that he achieved thanks to fasting, including having led his country to independence from the British empire without incurring major bloodshed. Even medicine and some therapies recommend it. Many doctors know that it is healthy to fast.

To discover the roots of this ancient practice in the Christian religion, we must look at the first disciples of Jesus and their writings about the life and culture of the first century. The "Didache," an old document written by the first disciples in or around 90 A.D., provides instructions to the Church of the first Christians: "You shouldn't fast on the same days as the hypocrites, for they fast on the second and fifth day of the week, you should instead fast on the fourth day and on the day of the preparation" (that is Good Friday, the *parasceve,* the day before Saturday, the Jewish Sabbath).

In Medjugorje, Our Lady brings us back to those days, asking us to fast on Wednesday and Friday ".... I would like the people to pray along with me these days. To pray as much as possible! To fast on Wednesdays and Fridays..." (Ivan Dragicevic, August 14, 1984). Isn't it wonderful to think that Our Lady wants to give us back this tradition of the early Church, that she herself lived? Like a good mother, she doesn't offer things to her children that she herself has not lived or put into practice.

The Blessed Mother didn't specifically explain why these two days in particular, but I had the opportunity to find out, thanks to the members of the prayer groups founded by her in Medjugorje, young people who were shaped by our Lady through the visionaries, over the course of many years. Let us not forget, that all that the Blessed Mother does has only one goal: to reveal Jesus. She comes for Jesus, to make us love Jesus, to bring us closer to the heart of Jesus.

Our Lady asked the prayer group that every Thursday of each week be a commemoration of the gift of the Eucharist and the Priesthood. Fasting on Wednesday and Friday is a way to commemorate this gift, a helpful reminder on Wednesdays that we should live Thursday with great love, and Friday calling to mind, with joy and faith, that Jesus gave his Body and Blood as food and drink, for us.

Wednesday. Our Mother Mary is so in love with the eucharist, the Bread of Life, that every Wednesday she prepares us for this commemoration of what is celebrated the next day. The Virgin Mary wants us to be free on Wednesday from the distraction of other foods, from grocery shopping, from cooking or any other concerns about food, in order to savor the bread that will become the true Body of Christ, since

Jesus himself chose the bread to be transformed into his Body. On Wednesday we shouldn't think: "good, tomorrow we can eat!" instead, we can fast with joy and with our heart; then we will enter into the mystery of the bread. Wouldn't it be so much more effective to prepare like the Jews in the desert during the exodus? God gave them manna, the bread that came down from heaven. The people, who would be the first to live the mystery of the eucharist, were being prepared. In the same way, Mary is preparing us today.

Thursday. On Thursday we commemorate with joy the institution of the Bread of Life. The Mass is at the center because Jesus is at the center! He burns with the desire to be our Divine food. Our Lady said: "Every week, live Thursday as if it were holy Thursday." On this day, let's celebrate in our heart, in a very special way, the gift of the Bread of Life that Jesus gave us at the Last supper. On Thursday, Jesus gave humanity the ultimate gift, the gift of himself in the Bread of Life. That's why He said: "I will be with you to the end of time." Jesus with his real presence is among us in all the tabernacles of the world. Every Thursday should be a very holy day, because on that day through the Eucharist, Jesus gave us his Body, Blood, soul and Divinity, to the end of the world. This day is priceless; it is the day of the Bread of Life.

Friday. Every time I hear the testimonies of the visionaries in Medjugorje, I'm astonished to hear that Our Lady never mentions fasting as a way to commemorate the death of Jesus on the cross. On the contrary, the Virgin Mary talks of Friday as the day that follows Thursday. The Queen of Peace doesn't want us to eat our favorite meal on Fridays, she asks us to hold as long as possible the taste of the bread, to remain immersed in the mystery of Christ. The Jews have a similar attitude towards the Sabbath, their most sacred day of the week. Each Saturday evening, at sunset, they extend the Sabbath by singing and reciting spiritual hymns. The Sabbath for the Jews is like their fiancée, they don't ever want to let her go! In the same way, by fasting on Friday, we continue to savor the bread that for us is the Bread of Life.

I often think of the Blessed Mother who remained on earth after the ascension among the apostles. Whenever she entered in the kitchens of the time, could she ever look at bread in the same way that she had looked at it before the Last supper? When she saw bread, her motherly heart must have skipped a beat, as she thought: "My son put himself in a piece of bread; here is the food that became my Son!"

When we consider that the bread is made out of grains of wheat, we have before our eyes the whole story of Jesus, the story of the Redeemer. When Jesus talks about the grain of wheat in the gospel, we see the sower and the grain of wheat that must die to produce abundant fruit one-hundredfold, some sixty, some thirty (Mt 13, 8). That's the whole history of the death and resurrection of Christ and of the fruits of redemption. In order for the grain of wheat to become bread, we need to grind it into flour, the essential element to make bread.

Jesus was crushed in His Body, His heart, His soul and in all his Divine Person. The grain of wheat embodies the love that Jesus has for us. He allowed himself to be crushed so that we could be nourished and become divinized. When Jesus talked of the Bread of Life He said: "If any one eats of this bread, he will live forever," (John 6: 51). This is the bread which came down from heaven. Your ancestors ate manna and died, but whoever feeds on this bread will live forever," (John 6: 58).

This is why we should face Wednesdays and Fridays with love for the bread, contemplating the history of our redemption. Our Lady desires that we immerse ourselves in this mystery, not only spiritually but also materially. Mary is a real Jewish woman. She immerses us into the bread to compel us to be with Jesus. Through fasting, Mary makes us focus on the presence and love of Jesus and allows us to be in awe with her, that Jesus, in His great humility, has become bread. This is the true meaning of fasting: love of the Eucharist. Jesus is always at the center of everything that our Lady tells and recommends to us. If we fast with love for the Bread of Life, our fast changes, it becomes joyful! That's why the Queen of Peace asks us to fast, but to fast with our heart. Our love for the Eucharist will become deeper. This is an amazing grace!

Marthe Robin, a great French mystic, said, "The glory that we will have in heaven is proportional to the fervor we have on earth for Holy Communion." In her messages, the Virgin Mary urges us to respect the teachings of the Catechism of the Catholic Church:

> "To prepare for worthy reception of this sacrament, the faithful should observe the fast required in their Church. Bodily de-

meanor (gesture, clothing) ought to convey the respect, solemnity, and joy of this moment when Christ becomes our guest."

The greater the devotion, love and gratitude with which we receive the Bread of Life, the greater our glory will be in heaven.

The Jewish tradition as well as the Christian tradition teaches us that fasting is a very powerful tool against Satan. Fasting is all the more important today as we struggle with the forces of evil. The Virgin Mary said in Medjugorje, "Dear children! Also, today I call you: live your vocation in prayer. Now, as never before, Satan wants to suffocate man and his soul by his contagious wind of hatred and unrest... hatred and war are growing from day to day..." (January 25, 2015).

We can see before our eyes the destruction that Satan has brought to the families, children and especially to the youth. The culture of death has put down roots in the western countries. In Medjugorje many pilgrims are distraught because their children are addicted to drugs, they live immoral lives or they are on their way to moral destruction. These parents ask the visionaries to pray that their children will stop using drugs or stop filling their emptiness with the distractions that come from the evil one. "Dear children! Today I call you to pray for my intentions. Renew fasting and prayer because Satan is cunning and attracts many hearts to sin and perdition," (October 25, 2012).

I remind them that the war that rages in the families and in the hearts of the youth, which our Lady talks about, is the same war that perhaps is ruining the lives of their children.

"Dear children, only with prayer and fasting can wars be stopped." When the Virgin Mary first appeared, she didn't speak of military warfare, but of wars within families. The Queen of Peace tells us: "When a war starts, it is because war is already in your hearts. But if you have peace in your heart, then the exterior war will stop immediately," (private message to Vicka during the gulf war in 1991).

Indeed, war starts in our hearts. If I feel hatred for my brother, if I close the door on this or that person, if I misjudge, condemn, or if I am jealous, or speak ill of others, if inside of me I have bitterness, it means that a war is in my heart and it will be transmitted to the outside and to those that I meet. These are the wars that the Virgin Mary wants to remove from our hearts! To achieve this, the only tools are fasting and prayer! If you want to try another method, go ahead, be warned though, it will leak water from all sides!

Let's not neglect these twin tools: prayer and fasting. Prayer is, was, and always has been an obvious and trustworthy tool in our tool belt. But let us not forget how much stronger this tool becomes when we pair it with fasting! We not only save lives, like the child who we dove into the icy river to save, but we can even improve our own health! Various studies show that people in the western world eat at least a third more than what they need. Many diseases and early deaths are caused by overeating. A bit of fasting will do us good.

You, parents who beg for the healing of your child, you, children who beg for the reconciliation of your parents, know that you have that power! Don't pray without fasting, and don't fast without praying. All the Saints obtained the graces they needed to be Saints, and they fasted. In the first weeks of the apparitions, the entire population listened attentively to every little word our Lady said. After about two months, Our Lady said: "Satan has a plan to destroy this parish. Dear children, I ask all the parishioners to fast on bread and water for three days and to pray the rosary in order to defeat Satan." And all in unison, everybody in the village did what the most holy Virgin Mary asked. For three days, with a united heart, they fasted and prayed that she could crush the snake's head. On the fourth day she said: "Dear children, I thank you for your prayers and your fasting, Satan's plan has failed, we won!" She didn't say: "I won." she said, "we won."

She needed those poor people in the parish of Medjugorje to defeat Satan. This is very important because without that sacrifice, Satan, in those days, would have realized his plan and today there would be no Medjugorje, there wouldn't be this river of blessings flowing on this earth for the past thirty-five years. Without Medjugorje, how many lives would have perished, how many families would not have reconciled, and how many young people would have committed suicide!

All of this because five hundred people in the village spent three days fighting against Satan. God, therefore, was able to give the gift of Medjugorje to the world, and to the millions of pilgrims that come to recharge their spiritual batteries. This is the impact of the one who says yes to fasting and prayer! In June of 1992 our Lady said to Ivanka: "Dear children, I ask you to win against Satan. The weapons are fasting and prayer. Pray for peace, because Satan wants to destroy the little peace that you have."

It is natural to ask: "She asks me to win against Satan? Who am I?" We are God's children and she needs you, me, each one of us, without exception. She says: "Dear children, without you I can't help the world" (August 28, 1986).

I remember that during the war in Bosnia - Herzegovina in 1992, we could hear the echo of the bombing in Mostar, Ljubuski, Citluk and in the countryside near Medjugorje. We could see the trail of bombs in the sky. The destruction and those who had been killed were shown daily on TV. By the grace of God, I was able to stay in Medjugorje, along with a few members of the Community of the Beatitudes. On April 25, 1992, Our Lady gave the first message since the beginning of the war. We were all eagerly waiting to know the Virgin Mary's answer to the ongoing tragedy that was around us. The words of our celestial Mother were: "Dear children! Only with prayer and fasting can war be stopped. Therefore, my dear little children, pray and by your life give witness that you are mine and that you belong to me, because Satan wishes in these turbulent days to seduce as many souls as possible. Therefore, I invite you to decide for God and he will protect you and show you what you should do and which path to take." The Virgin Mary had said this before the war; she had to repeat it.

# 3. Our Body

Why does fasting weaken Satan so much? When we offer God something that touches our body, we can truly say that we give ourselves. It is one thing to give money, time, a good word, or our services, but fasting affects something vital. Food is a matter of survival. It affects our profound ontological and metaphysical habits.

Father Slavko Barbaric, a Franciscan priest in the village from the beginning of the apparitions until his death in 2000, and also a trained psychiatrist, used to say: "Fasting reveals our dependencies." When we fast on bread and water, a series of flashing signals light up: Coffee! Cigarettes! Wine! Chocolate! The Blessed Mother doesn't come to point out our attachments, to blame, to make us feel bad. She comes so that by becoming aware of our daily dependencies we can be freed from them. We realize to what extent we have become creatures or slaves of habits and daily routine. Certainly, routine has its positive side, isn't virtue after all a good habit? When disordered however, routine can be used to persevere in sinful practices, to the point that it becomes almost impossible to get out of; this is the case of vices. Newspapers and television are devious addictions, we don't even realize the cluttering effect they have on us. To Jelena's prayer group Our Lady said, "In addition to food, it would be a good thing to give up television, because after seeing some programs, you are distracted and unable to pray. You can also give up alcohol, cigarettes, and other pleasures. You yourselves know what you have to do" (December 8, 1981).

When I started fasting on bread and water, my first discovery was the joy it gave me of being free from food. It didn't matter whether I ate or not. During their missions, it did not matter to the apostles whether they had time to eat or not. Their utmost concern was working intensely for God. The giving of our bodies is a sign of having really given ourselves to God. Fr Slavko used to say: "Fasting allows the soul to govern the body and not the other way around."

Fasting creates a vacuum that creates a space in our souls, in our bodies and in our hearts. When we are not worried about eating, we free a space for God to dwell in us as never before. Our heart is already big enough to hold God himself, but fasting allows God to extend the boundaries of our heart and encompass all of the heavenly dimensions. The holy spirit can dwell in this new interior territory. This is why those who fast have a special sharpness and spiritual sensitivity. They are more inspired than those who don't fast.

At the request of Our Lady, an English woman founded a community in England. One day I asked her if Our Lady had requested that their members fast.

"Yes," she answered. "Our Lady asked us to fast every day."

"Every day?" I gasped. "That's impossible!" "Yes, we fast every day from 4:00 to 6:00 P.M."

I laughed to myself and seeing the smirk on my face she explained, "we British have grown up having our tea-time from 4:00 to 6:00 P.M. every afternoon."

By taking teatime away from an Englishman, his identity is affected — he is detached from his childhood traditions and his national identity.

A friend of mine from Mexico once told me that she stopped fasting during one of her pregnancies, and picked it up again a year later. She told me that during that year there was something missing in the communication between her and her children, the ability to explain to them the realities of life. They were not listening to her in the same way. As soon as she started fasting again, she felt she was immediately inspired by the holy spirit. The holy spirit brought to her mind the right words for her to say to her children and the children listened to her with their hearts. This is a nice example of how our fasting invites the holy spirit to occupy this new space that has been created in our heart and takes over. It is like an additional residence for the Trinity that we offer to God so that he can dwell in us.

Fasting is a preparation for the great works of God and the fulfilment of his will for us and the whole world. I had the great privilege to meet Father Zdenko, a holy Franciscan Priest who lived in Siroki Brieg, on the outskirts of Medjugorje. He is now dead. I attended his funeral where there were thousands of people who loved him not only because he had a great gift of healing, but also because he was able to read peoples' hearts. When he was alive his fame spread to all the countries of the former Yugoslavia, and people came from far away for a simple blessing from him. He didn't offer a solution to a problem; he was actually quite abrupt in his ways. If someone had a problem, he blessed him and the conversation ended there. He slept on the floor and fasted a lot. Thanks to his ascetic life and his immense love for God he obtained many graces from the Lord.

# 4. Prepare the Great Works of God

Ivica, one of my friends from Medjugorje, told me that her grandmother, a childhood friend of Father Zdenko, shared with her the following event.

One day the Lord, speaking to this humble friar, told him: "Zdenko, would you accept to fast on bread and water for seven years?" Fr. Zdenko accepted and fasted for seven years. On the last day of the seventh year, the Lord spoke with him again and asked: "Zdenko, would you accept adding an eighth year to your fast?" Father Zdenko again accepted. Guess what day that was? Incredible! The last day of the eight year was exactly June 24, 1981, the date of the first apparition of Our Lady in Medjugorje! Do you understand the grandeur of what happened? Who is able in some way to know how God prepares his great works? We shall find out only in heaven!

Here is another testimony related to this Franciscan: another time, they brought him an alcoholic lady. Nothing had ever worked to rid her of alcoholism. Father Zdenko received her and told her: "You should not drink. Do you promise not to drink anymore?" When she promised, Father Zdenko blessed her in the name of the Father, the son and the holy spirit, and the woman returned home. The next day, and the following day she did not drink, but on the third day it was particularly hot and the temptation to drink increased more and more. Then she took a cup, filled it with wine, and as she brought the cup close to her lips, she saw a finger on the cup and heard the voice of Father Zdenko who, scolding her, said: "I have told you not to drink anymore!" Shocked, she immediately dropped the cup and it broke into a million pieces. The woman was healed and didn't drink again for the rest of her days.

# 5. Protection

Protection is another marvelous fruit of fasting. What parent doesn't wish to protect their children and grandchildren? Today, they have life and health insurance, but life insurance has never prevented anyone from dying! Besides, accident insurance only works when an accident has happened! And even in the end there is always the small print stating that we can't be reimbursed. Instead, "fasting insurance" works before a misfortune occurs; it thus prevents us from a misfortune. The Virgin Mary in fact teaches us that, if we help her by fasting, she can keep Satan far from us!

I must admit that I get very angry when I hear certain people say, "we don't have to see Satan everywhere, we are not even sure he exists!" In her Messages, the Queen of Peace reminds us that Satan exists and her teachings cover four main points: 1) Satan exists; 2) today he is stronger than ever before; 3) he is always at work; 4) his main goal is not only to destroy all that is holy in us, but to also destroy "nature and the planet on which we live." The Queen of Peace also tells us, "Dear children, see how through humble prayer, we can disarm him?" She used the word "we," referring to herself and us, her children. If I were the mother of ten children, and I knew that a Satanist was wandering outside, wanting to torture, rape and kill, I would absolutely feel it my duty to warn them. If I didn't do so or if I would tell them: "Don't worry, you can play in the forest, you'll be fine." Well, I would be responsible for the murder of my babies. One has no right to hide from children the fact that spiritual warfare exists, that it is not only the good God who acts, but there is also an enemy who acts and he too lives in a place. It is called hell. Jesus didn't come to die on the Cross as a joke! He came to free us from evil and eternal condemnation! And much less is it a joke that he has invited his Mother to Medjugorje for so many years, to warn us that it is time to convert, because evil is for real! We have an enemy who is sadistic, who threatens us, and we must take light and guidance from the Messages of the Queen of Peace. This is why our Lady tells us: "Dear children, I invite all in the world, in a special way, to prayer and renunciation, because now as never before, Satan wants to seduce as many people as possible into the way of death and sin" (September 25, 1991).

And she has her reasons to warn us! After all, it has been so from the beginning, and even St. Peter tells us: "Be sober, watch your enemy. The devil, like a roaring lion, goes about seeking someone to devour" (1 Pt 5, 8). Today, the number of suicides is greater than ever: even wars, tumors, and highway accidents kill less people than suicides. With prayer and fasting we can intervene and protect not only ourselves but everyone else. Through prayer and fasting we are able to find protection. "Pray as much as you can," the Queen of Peace tells us. "Fast, persevere in prayer and sacrifices, and I will protect you and will hear your prayers." She knows well that we are in need of being protected! She tells us: "Dear children, with your help, I can do everything." Do we really think about it? When we pray to Our Lady, do we really believe that she can do everything? Often, we behave as if we don't have a Powerful God, able to truly help us. If Mary says that with our help she can do everything, it is because the Power of God himself works in her!

# 6. Purification from Evil

The Queen of Peace invites us to give to God all the evil that has piled up in us to purify us from all past sins. Only through prayer are we able to recognize what is evil and give it to God, so that he can completely purify our hearts. To obtain that, we are invited to pray constantly and to prepare our hearts through penance and fasting.

We commit sin at the moment we are of age to do so and these accumulate. Despite having confessed, we carry upon us the consequences. Our Lady says that with her prayers, she will help us to free ourselves from the consequences of our past sins. We should, therefore, give the bad past to God. When a child falls and is hurt, the mother cares for and alleviates the consequences of his fall. There is the Blood of Christ that washes us from sin, but the mother helps us repair the wounds. Indeed, she is truly a mother to all of us! By fasting, we are inviting the Madonna to heal us. She will know how to heal at a deeper level and our wounds will heal faster.

By fasting, we permit God to remove all moral filth that may have grown in us. It is this filth that weighs us down and makes us sad, depressed and incapable of loving. Then, when the Lord comes, and with the holy spirit, He removes this filth, and we suddenly become able to love our neighbor, who earlier we couldn't in any way stand! By means of fasting, in effect, we allow the holy spirit to increase his Power in our hearts.

# 7. Fasting is Powerful

Many people have removed from their lives Our Lady's message on fasting. In fact it is the message, given by Our Lady, which most people ignore. Often, I hear: "It is very hard for me, I am very attached to food, I don't want to force myself to do it."

One of the benefits of fasting is that it wards off the demons. Therefore, it's normal that they will do everything they can to distract us from practicing it and convince us that it is reserved for those people who are "already holy," and to whom we surely don't belong.

I had the opportunity to ask Father Amorth, the famous exorcist, this question directly: "Father, how do you explain the incredible power of fasting over evil and the demons?" Father responded loudly in his unmistakable tone: "Because fasting costs us! Yes, fasting is hard!" Father then continued: "At Fatima, and now in Medjugorje, our Lady often insists on prayer and fasting. And this is even more important today since humanity is under the influence of consumerism. Humanity tries at all costs to avoid sacrifice, exposing itself to sin. To live a Christian life, in addition to prayer, we need to live in sobriety: without sobriety, there is no perseverance. I give an example: today families separate with extreme ease. Marriage takes place, then inevitably they get divorced. This happens because we are not disposed to sacrifice. now to be able to live together, we must be capable of even accepting the defects of the other. This lack of sacrificial spirit comes from the fact that we don't live completely like Christians. Just look with what superficiality abortions are carried out, that implies that we are not ready to make the sacrifice to educate children. Here we have the prime motive for failing marriages: we are no longer used to sacrifice. Only through exercising sacrifice ourselves, are we capable of living a Christian life."

Jesus himself, in the gospels, gives us an enlightening answer, remember? Jesus invites his apostles to go before him to preach, drive out demons, heal the sick, raise the dead, announce the good news, etc...one day they were joyful and excited to tell Jesus: "Lord, even the demons submit to us in your name," (Lk 10.17).

It is easy to understand their joy in witnessing the enemy being defeated and expelled from tortured hearts, and seeing the demons fleeing from those in agony.

*Father Gabriele Amorth, Presidente Onorario*
*Associazione Internazionale Esorcisti*

On another occasion, the apostles returned to Jesus after one of their missions, but this time remained silent, undoubtedly a little disappointed by their failure. The father of a child, in fact, turned to Jesus, making him aware that his disciples were not able to cast out the evil spirit from his son, and he asked why. Jesus responded: "This type of demon cannot be cast out in any way but through prayer and fasting" (Mt 17.21). The answer of Jesus is glaring, crystal clear and irrefutable! When Jesus points out specific demons by saying, "this type" we can only imagine that it refers to very evil and cruel spirits of the highest order. They are the ones who cannot be defeated solely by the prayer of the apostles with the name of Jesus.

In fact, as with the angels and Saints, a hierarchy exists with demons too and this explains the different degrees of evil and harm they can do. For "this type," which has a greater resistance to the disciples, a strong and potent remedy is necessary along with prayer: fasting.

As for us, if we choose to pray and fast, then fasting will demand from us some sacrifice, especially at the beginning, when it becomes necessary to break with long standing eating habits. I therefore make a special effort each week to fast, so as to close the door to the demons so that they cannot harm me. These demons are disarmed and cannot attack me and so I can enjoy a great peace.

Through fasting, we prevent suffering and we confound the evil plans that the demons plot against us, our families, our health. So therefore, I do everything within my power, nothing less, with all my heart, and let the Lord do the rest.

At this point I want to ask you a question: would you prefer to put up with the sacrifice of fasting, or to be made the target of immense sufferings generated by these invisible and malicious enemies who are the demons? As for me, I have made my choice. I have suffered in the past many times because of the demons, particularly when I was following occult practices in my youth. Such sufferings were unbearable as is well known by those who are tormented by demons. In comparison to this torment, the effort to fast is like a gentle caress!

And "don't forget the blessing!" Mary says. Among both the Jews and holy Christians, they do not dare to eat food without blessing it first. Saying a brief prayer over your bread attracts many graces over you, your fast and your health. Saint Bernadette used a straightforward method. She traced a cross over the bread with her hand and said: "If God is here, may he remain. If Satan is here, may he leave!" But each person can find their own words. For example: "Come Lord, bless this bread you give us through your Bounty, fruit of the earth and work of human hands, that it will give us the strength to serve you. Oh Lord, give bread to those who are hungry."

The term "fasting" is present in the Vulgate of St. Jerome ("hoc autemgenua non elicitor nisi per orationem et ielunium"). This passage in the gospel exists in various other original documents in the Greek language. Some refer to fasting, others do not. If some passages don't mention it, we can still be sure that Jesus did speak about it. In the same way, we look at who was present at the foot of the cross when Jesus was crucified: some evangelists say Mary Magdalen was present, others do not. It suffices that one says she was to believe that Mary Magdalen was present.

# 8. A Battlefield

Why does our Lady invite us repeatedly to fast two days a week? Because she is a mother and her maternal love surpasses all earthly intensity. Our Lady knows well that today her children live on a battlefield, be it in the temporal or spiritual realms, and she doesn't hide this reality from us. "Today, like never before," she tells us: "Satan wants to destroy all that is holy in you. He wants to destroy your families, nature and even the planet on which you live. Satan wants war." Finding yourself on a battlefield, without knowing either the identity of your enemy or his methods of destruction, is to advance without being equipped with the right weapons. It means walking on a minefield with a total disregard of the risk you are running, condemning yourself to defeat. If, on the contrary, we listen to the voice of Jesus in the gospel, as affirmed by Our Lady in Medjugorje, we will use the right weapons, wearing the impenetrable armor of prayer and fasting to defeat the enemy.

Some people reading my books tell me that this is difficult advice to accept. But, is it the advice that is difficult, or rather, the actual evolution of our society? Certainly nothing is automatic with God, we are not saved simply because we fast. But, let's look around, where is the world heading? aren't we already in a state of emergency? Even Our Lady herself, who always thinks of positive and encouraging words to say to us, told us on September 2, 2011, that "everything is falling apart." In a state of emergency, we need an emergency plan: to rescue an injured person on the road, a welcomed emergency call is made right away. But for wounded souls like ours? Father Slavko Barbaric, a holy priest from Medjugorje, who deeply understood why fasting is desired by Our Lady, wanted us to consider the following: "Let us suppose you are invited for a meal with your friends and must strictly follow a diet due to a bad case of diabetes. Your friends will accept, in good faith, the fact that you are abstaining from eating sweets or other delicious foods, so as not to provoke a harmful crisis. They wouldn't take issue with this dietary requirement. Likewise, at home, you must abstain daily, morning and night, from eating foods that you used to enjoy, but that today threatens the health of your body."

And what about the health of our souls which are called to eternal Life? Isn't there perhaps a need to protect them with infinite care? And what about the health of millions of other souls, who don't yet know the love of God, wandering aimlessly? Isn't it therefore worth it to fast, so that they may also find the light?

Seeing that St. Macarius of Egypt (Fourth Century hermit) fasted and worked very much, some of his contemporaries wanted to control him, but to them he responded: "Leave me in peace, this is how I torment those who nag me!"

# 9. Givers or Takers?

Our choices reveal the depth of our commitment to follow Jesus and to serve our neighbor.

For example, business people show different degrees of involvement in their work: some choose to give themselves to the max and be zealous in the very sense of the word, doing an excellent job; others, while being active, are less motivated. Others, in short, work only for their own gain and don't take to heart the future of the organization they work for.

The same thing happens in the spiritual life: there are those who take to heart the fate of the whole Church, they work hard so that Christ will be known and loved, whatever may be the position they hold in the Christian community, they do their work whole heartedly, and give themselves completely. These are the Saints, known and unknown, without whom the future of the Church would be uncertain. On the other hand, there are others who work in a less radical way, and finally, there are those who give a few hours of their time to fulfill a duty for the community, but without putting their souls into it.

Surely, it is necessary to say that the degree of commitment doesn't depend on what's done, but in the way it's done. Mother Teresa of Calcutta said in this regard: "What's important is not to do great things, but to do them with great love."

In the practice of fasting, the same scale of motivation exists. True, it is possible to go to heaven without having fasted, living all the same an authentic Christian life. There are still those few who sometimes are protected while never having fasted. However, we should at least ask ourselves: who has fasted for them? Who loves them so much as to have them in their hearts to make sacrifice for them and for their salvation? For how many thousands of sinners did the Curé of Ars fast? And when St Faustina Kowalska fasted, to the extent in which the vow of obedience would allow her (she changed her cell so that no one would notice), did she know that millions of Christians and non-Christians would benefit from her sacrifices and her holiness? Did she know that through her writings, inspired by Divine Mercy, millions of sinners would be immersed in God's embrace?

With this extraordinary freedom, which God has given us, we choose the degree of commitment we want to employ in the coming of God's Kingdom on earth. We can choose to be givers or takers.

Have you guessed who is infinitely happy here on earth and who in heaven?

# 10. Facing Disastrous Paths, is There a Solution?

I often meet parents worried about their children who have embarked on a disastrous path, especially those experimenting with drugs. They are parents who pray fervently, who make pilgrimages and say a multitude of novenas, but on the other hand, they are also very discouraged seeing that often, things don't improve. They ask me to pray and to have the visionaries in Medjugorje pray for their intentions. I reassure them by saying to them their prayers already have a great merit in the eyes of God. Then I ask them this decisive question: "But do you fast for your child?" and they say: "No, sister, but we pray a lot!" I ask: "good, but why don't you fast?" They tell me: "Uh …in reality, we can't give up food, sister!" and I say: "I understand but are you willing for the salvation of your child, to add fasting to your prayers?" and after a moment of silence they often conclude by telling me: "Agreed, we will fast for him/her."

The visionary, Ivan Dragicevic, spoke about the future of the Church and the world. On August 14, 2012, Ivan was interviewed on Radio Maria by Father Livio Fanzaga. here is an extract of the interview upon which we can reflect! "When the secrets of the Gospa are revealed in Medjugorje, the Catholic Church will find itself living through a great trial concerning the world and the faithful, and a little of that suffering is already underway."

"Today, Satan is stronger than ever and wants primarily to destroy families and the youth because they make up the foundation of a new world. Presidents and rulers of nations receive their power from God, but many of them use it for their own interests. The result is a chaotic society. Without God, the world has no future. Our Lady invites us to return to God and to walk with him towards the future, thus ensuring peace and harmony. A government without God is anarchy, a government of deceit.

For this reason, it is important that God is present in the rule of nations and that he be put in the first place. Where conscience is missing, peace is continuously threatened. The cruelest war is the one that breaks out in the heart of man, in which the void of God has allowed Satan a very ample range of action."

Ivan then asked the listeners to pray, so that Mary's plans may be fulfilled.

During a meeting with pilgrims in Medjugorje, Ivan said: "The main targets of Satan are families and the youth, his second aim is to destroy the Church and priests. He wants to prevent the flourishing of priestly vocations."[1] The trials we know today could have been avoided!

But future ones can still be avoided! Because Our Lady also says: "Dear children, with fasting and prayer you can obtain everything," (October 15, 1983 Jelena Vasilj).

---

[1] Ivan received from Our Lady the mission to pray for priests and families. Each Thursday when Ivan is there, Medjugorje opens its chapel to the priests who wish to pray with him during the time of the apparition.

# 11. The Suggestions of Satan

When we make room for God through fasting, the devil is cast out. Jesus frees us from our past sins, and Our Lady repairs the damage that has been caused, and clothes us with new beauty! Clearly, this makes Satan very angry.

Our Lady warned the prayer group in 1983: "Be prudent because Satan tempts all who have made the decision to consecrate themselves to God. He will suggest, to those that pray and fast much, that you should become like other young people and go in search of pleasures. Do not listen to him or obey him! When you become strengthened in faith, the demon will not be able to seduce you," (16 June, 1983).

We should remain alert to this fight. Satan's seductions are very subtle! Our Lady reproached us for not being aware of this. What will Satan do when he sees that we have made the decision to fast? He will suggest: "Fast two days a week? That's too much! you will be isolated from your family and friends! And on those days, you won't look well, you will be pale and drawn. Cook yourself a steak instead, it will do you good. God doesn't want you to become weak, but if you fast you will feel very weak. Do like everybody else, they don't worry about these things. Enjoy life and eat whatever you want; relax and chill out!"

But Jesus never once mentioned in the gospels: "Do like everybody else." When you hear phrases like that, you can be sure of its origin. The best way to put yourself into the hands of Satan is to "do like everybody else." In fact, what does the world do?

When Satan tempts us, we often make the mistake of responding to him. If he tells us, "You should eat, see how pale you are! Just eat!" We must not respond: "I want to fast. Don't you see how ugly you are? Get away from me!" Don't do this; we must never converse with Satan. If he disturbs us, let us speak to God instead: "Lord, Satan is bothering me, please do something!" Satan will outsmart us and trick us if we engage in a conversation with him. This is how Eve was fooled. If instead of speaking with Satan she had said: "Lord, the serpent is telling me the contrary of what you have said, what should I do?" For sure she would not have eaten the apple!

Fasting bears much fruit when we do it with all our heart. Often, on Wednesday and Friday mornings, we do not feel in the mood to fast. But if we enter into the spirit of fasting, with love for the Bread of Life, placing Jesus in first place, we succeed in fasting with the heart because we love Jesus!

Our Lady has said: "Dear children! Today I call on you to begin fasting with the heart. There are many people who are fasting, but only because everyone else is fasting. It has become a custom which no one wants to stop. I ask the parish to fast out of gratitude because God has allowed me to stay this long in this parish. Dear children, fast and pray with the heart. Thank you for having responded to my call," (20 September, 1984).

Fasting should become a thanksgiving for the Eucharist and for the presence of our Lady among us.

# 12. Until the Completion of the Plan

We all want to fully live the vocation that God put in our hearts when he created us and we desire that his plan for us is accomplished before we die. We want to hear the Lord tell us: "I am pleased because you allowed me to accomplish all that I planned for you!"

In 1985 Our Lady said: "Dear children, I wish to tell you to renew the messages which I am giving you. Especially live the fast, because by fasting you will achieve and cause me the joy of the whole plan, which God is planning here in Medjugorje, being fulfilled" (26 September, 1985).

When she speaks about the plan for Medjugorje, she speaks about the plan for each of our lives. Through fasting, we permit God to fully realize the project he has for us, our family and our city. Let us permit God to fully achieve his plan. When he created us, he believed in us! When we pray, we hope that God will respond to our prayers. Likewise, when God looks at us, he hopes that the seeds that he planted in the depths of our heart will grow, so much so that, with the help of his grace, we will open like a flower and fulfill our potential to become a Saint. By fasting we have the potential to fully realize God's plan for us. Do you want God to grant all of your prayers? here is the message that will open new horizons for you: "Prayer is the only way that brings peace. If you persevere in prayer and fasting, you will obtain all that you pray for" (15 October, 1983).

Saying 'yes' to fasting is very powerful. God will never ask for things that we are not able to accomplish. For example, when you are ill, no one expects you to play football, but if you feel ill, you can still say yes by offering your suffering to Jesus. And this is most effective. If someone is in sin, he can decide for conversion. Although the grace of God has no limits, God still requires our yes. In this way, he can spread abundant blessings over the whole world. Only when we reach heaven will we find out that, thanks to fasting, thanks to our yes to the request of Our Lady, hundreds of thousands of young people have avoided suicide, many young couples have not divorced, and many babies have not been aborted. Who can know the power of our yes? Now, let us say yes and begin!

# 13. Purgatory

What an incredible act of mercy fasting on bread and water is for those who can't pray for themselves! The people who have preceded us, and who are in purgatory, suffer very much. In 1982 Our Lady spoke to the visionaries about the souls in Purgatory and said: "The souls in Purgatory await your prayers and sacrifices" (2 November, 1982).

When we lose a close friend or relative, it is beautiful to take flowers to the cemetery, put their photo on our nightstand, remember all the good things he or she did for us, but all these things do not help them. if we want them to leave quickly the atrocious sufferings of Purgatory, we must fast for them. This act of free and perfect love creates a marvelous bond between the living and the dead and frees the souls from their agony.

Of course, our Lady told us that the Mass is an extraordinary means to release souls from Purgatory, but...don't forget she also asked us to fast!

# 14. Choosing to be Healed

Our Lady has spoken a lot about healing. Many pilgrims look for her intercession and ask the visionaries to pray for their loved sick ones. She takes them very much to heart! In almost all the nightly apparitions on the mountain, Ivan tells us that the Gospa prays particularly for the sick and for those we carry in our hearts. She is very close to those who suffer in body and soul. Oh, if the sick would know how the Blessed Mother favors them, they would be greatly consoled. Truly in them, she sees her suffering Son. Think of the compassion and ardent love of Saint Camillus of Lellis for the sick, or that of so many other Saints, including doctors like Saint Giuseppe Moscati. There is a compassion so well demonstrated by them, to the point of shedding tears for their patients or giving everything up for their sick brothers. And yet this is nothing in comparison to what Our Lady does for her children. Besides, the Immaculate Mother knows well that sickness is not part of God's original plan, but is instead the fruit of corruption.

Our Lady tells us that to obtain healing for sickness, it is good to recite seven our Father's, Hail Mary's and glory Be's and to fast on bread and water. Furthermore, on June 23, 1985, she gave Jelena this prayer to recite with the heart when any of our dear ones are ill:

Prayer for the sick: "Oh my God, this person who is ill before you, has come to ask you that which he wishes and holds most dear to him. You, oh God, make this word enter his heart: 'The health of the soul is important!' Lord, may your holy will be done in everything! If you wish him to be healed, grant him health. But if your will differs, so that he continues to carry his cross, I also pray for us, who intercede for him; purify our hearts to become worthy to transmit your holy mercy. Oh, God, protect him and relieve his suffering, may your holy will be done in him. Through him may your holy name be revealed. Help him carry his cross with courage."

Our Lady has said: "This is the most beautiful prayer you can recite for a person who is ill."

When someone in our family is ill, we spend much time preoccupied in looking for the best doctor, the best medicine, the most renowned specialist. We do everything in order to save the life of the ill person. When we then see this suffering in a child, we go through tooth and nail and spend a fortune to save his life. But it is easier than we think, as we begin to do our part through praying and fasting. In many cases, prayer and fasting obtains the miraculous healing of the one who is ill. Responding to a question about a particular sick person, mentioned to her, the Gospa said: "Have a firm faith, pray and fast and be healed. Trust and remain joyful. Be patient and pray for healing," (November 26, 1981).

And the anointing of the sick? This sacrament of the Catholic Church obtains, in some cases, the healing of the sick, but in all cases peace of heart. Let us not wait until the sick person is at the point of death to call a priest, with the stole and the holy oil. At this sight, the sick person could die of fear! Instead, when the illness becomes serious, call a priest and begin to fast for the sick person. Such a sacrament is expressly called "the last rites," clearly not such an appropriate term. This word "last" may give the impression to the sick person that he is going to die and he might be afraid of that. Whereas, after receiving the anointing of the sick, he may live many more years and receive many more sacraments.

One day a lady, ill with a tumor, came to see me and told me: "My problem is that in my family no one believes and no one prays or fasts for me." I replied that we would do it for her family. To this day, this is a common problem that can still be resolved easily. In families that don't pray, visit those who are ill, talk with them about the Lord, announce to them the good news, and tell them that you will pray and fast. When the visionaries asked Our Lady if she had healed this or that ill person, she would often remind them that she can't heal, but that only God is able to do so. What she wants us to do is to pray and at the same time she promises to pray for us. The only thing we need to do is to believe firmly, fast, do penance and God will come to the rescue of all his children. "For the healing of an illness a firm faith is necessary, constant prayer accompanied by an offering of fasting and sacrifice. I can't help those who don't pray and don't make sacrifices. also, those who are in good health should pray and fast for those who are ill" (August 18, 1982).

Then when healing doesn't come, it means God has another plan and doesn't stop granting his blessings to the person who is ill. Even in that case we pray and the Blessed Mother will grant us new eyes to see and receive, God's will, with love.

Think of Zelie and Louis Martin, the parents of St. Theresa, now Saints. They realized that Zelie's illness was hopeless and all available cures were not working out, they decided to go to Lourdes with their three older daughters. The hope that got that Saintly family going was immense, embellished with an even bigger confidence. Zelie always took care to remind her children that what is important is God's will: pray without doubting, and to be ready to accept the possibility of returning home without being healed! Unfortunately, nothing happened in Lourdes, so even with repeated dousing with blessed water obtained during the pilgrimage, this didn't save Zelie...but you will agree with me that the story of that family would be very different, if the five daughters would not all have entered religious life and...perhaps the Church would have one less Doctor!

God had prepared for her a special place in heaven. He has assigned to us, and the Virgin Mary knows this well, which thrones each one of his children will sit on! God the Father is ready to risk us suffering a little upon this earth just to see that place occupied by us and, once there, when seated on our throne, we will be the first to thank him for not having granted that which we asked for. Let us not doubt anymore, that trials will merit a great glory. And when it is our loved one's turn to suffer, our son for example, let us ask our Lady to watch over him from heaven, to help us wish for our loved ones who are ill, the greatest glory possible. Let's do the math, eternity is very, very much longer!

# 15. Fasting for Children

When I speak about fasting to children, I explain to them, with examples, what it means to make a sacrifice. I tell them that the Virgin Mary passes by each home every evening, takes all the sacrifices that are done during the day and puts them in a basket. Then I ask them to close their eyes and think of what sacrifice they will offer to Our Lady when she passes by that evening. Behold, I see them closing their little eyes tightly, concentrating in prayer and joyfully saying: I got it!

It is incredible to observe how much children know about being generous! This is not about making children fast on bread and water two days a week. It will, however, be important for them to see their parents fasting. I am sure they will be immediately overwhelmed by their questions: "Why fast?" "Me too!" and, "I also want to make a sacrifice!" Then they will give up candies, ice cream, they will not eat their favorite goodies, they will do without TV and video-games.

In fact, there is no limit to their capacity to love and to give to others. They are the ones that teach us to be generous! I have met couples who renounced divorce thanks to the sacrifices and prayers of their children. They are quite intelligent and know very well the effort it takes. They can do without a cookie, an ice cream, and to finish eating all they have on their plate. They can control their language, and maybe you'll discover that they use only one word rather than ten. These are the sacrifices that prepare them to fast on bread and water.

Clare, a little five-year-old girl, during the rosary with her parents and older brother, never failed to make it to the fifth Mystery without falling asleep. A religious sister very close to the family, told the story of how to console Jesus during the days leading up to Christmas, and she gave her a gift of a small wooden cradle with hay: each day she could add a piece of straw for each sacrifice she made. The little one was very happy, on the 25th of December she would be able to place Baby Jesus on real straw! One morning after receiving such a splendid gift, while she was going to school, she told her Mom: "Mommy, today I will say the whole rosary." In the evening, while everyone was ready to say the rosary, the mother saw the little one kneel in front of the statue of our Lady and stay there, in the same position for all five Mysteries. At the end of the rosary, the child, very happy, said: "Tonight I will put three straws for Baby Jesus, one because I said the entire rosary, one because I said it on my knees and one because I forgave my brother!"

Of course, we must be aware that children can be very clever and mischievous. My six-year-old nephew, Francis, discovered a great trick. One evening he came to the table, saw some food that he did not like and after the blessing declared solemnly to his father: "Pop, today I am fasting!"

His father responded: "Good, as a fast, offer the sacrifice of eating all that you don't like!"

# 16. Suspending the Laws of Nature

The Queen of Peace has said more than once: "Through fasting and prayer you can stop war and suspend the laws of nature."

We don't pay enough attention to this message. This means that disasters such as floods, earthquakes and landslides can be avoided if someone in the city, threatened by a catastrophe, would fast.

This message applies also to the laws of nature of our body. I know an American nurse, absorbed in a sinful life, who threw herself into the arms of the first man she would find. As a child, she frequented Catechism, but, growing up she preferred to put aside God and his Commandments. In the hospital where she worked there was a doctor who, years earlier in Medjugorje, radically converted. Upon returning home, he started to live the messages of the Blessed Mother with all his heart. Feeling inside that this nurse needed help, despite not having a special bond with her, he decided freely to fast for her, and her conversion.

He fasted for four years. One day, out of desperation, this lady decided to commit suicide. Being a nurse, she knew the right dose of tablets to take to obtain a sure death. She swallowed her medicines and went to bed, awaiting death.

The next morning, she awoke fresh as a daisy, without any discomfort! It was as if she drank a good glass of milk! She was shocked.

She was so amazed to be alive that she started saying: "Someone doesn't want me to die. surely then God exists and wants me to live! Reflecting upon God, she came to this conclusion: "Maybe God loves me."

Returning to work she felt almost obliged to tell the story to this same doctor. It was then that the doctor became fully aware of the effect of his fast. In fact, through this, God was able to do miracles in the life of the nurse. The doctor took this occasion to speak about God with her, an unthinkable thing before the suicide attempt, and her heart opened to the merciful love of God. She quickly understood that the doctor's fast had blocked the laws of nature and chemicals of the medicines in her body.

The doctor advised her to go to Medjugorje. It was here that our Lady showed her great love and even appeared to her. She couldn't believe that the Mother of God would appear to a sinner like her. Immediately the nurse fell in love with Mary and went to confession. She confessed all her sins and from that day on her life changed. Today, she has become an apostle of Our Lady in the United states and recognizes being 'born' in Medjugorje.

# 17. Satan Doesn't Give Gifts

I have already explained that fasting obtains many more healings than we think, and instead of running directly to a hundred doctors we would do well to fast and pray.

Unfortunately, many people (it is even said that thirteen million Italians) call on 'healers,' yoga or reiki masters and magicians, for the purpose of alleviating symptoms of all sorts of ailments. However, you need to know that one day these fake healers received their gift, and from God knows who.

In the Community of the Beatitudes, we often help to repair the damage of these so-called miracle 'healers,' a sort of after-sales service! When people go the healer, if they have a bad left knee for example, it may be that their knee heals, but what they don't know is that the ailment has simply shifted. It will strike another organ and will become even more severe. These people then return to the healer who will conjure other spells, and perhaps he will heal this second pain; but a third evil will arise elsewhere, worse than before, and one day they will awake with unspeakable anguish, driven to suicide, a death wish. How come all of a sudden, it turns out one discovers a young man hanging from a rope, while nothing apparently justifies this act on his part? In many cases it is later found that the mother had taken him as a baby to some 'healer.'

The healer pronounces some strange words (sometimes mixed with Christian prayers), often using secret formulas where, coincidentally, he is designated as Judas the traitor, and performs massages. An ex-healer, who renounced doing 'healings,' after converting, confided to me that he received his 'powers' from another person, who received them from still another, so, looking to trace the origin of this 'gift,' one finds that at the source of all this is a sorcerer who has received his gift directly from Satan! Do not be fooled, Satan just pretends to heal, trying to imitate the healings done by Jesus. Jesus tells us in the gospels that in the latter times false prophets will make extraordinary signs and wonders, for the purpose of seducing the elect, if it were possible. It is real! And because Satan doesn't give gifts, he does nothing more than shift the disease, making it worse.

Therefore, those who turn to healers never heal. On the contrary, they continue to become ill and the sickness passes from the body to the heart and from the heart to the soul. Starting from only a physical illness, it develops all of a sudden into a temptation to commit suicide, incredible hatred, deep depression. One day you can't take your own husband anymore, his way of speaking, of walking, of eating. Suddenly, you can't pray anymore and you have lost the joy of living, you are stunned, you are unable to arise in the morning and to do your own work, you can't move any longer and have terrible headaches. The result of this 'bad medicine' affects your children as well. It is not only a physical ailment, but also a lack of motivation. There is an inward emptiness. I beg you to not consult healers!

Our Lady has often spoken about going to doctors but never to go to healers. Why? Because you know very well who is behind them! Healers have caused many deaths, many suicides, and much mental illness. It is my duty to tell you: don't go to healers, even if they offer to heal you for free, even if they have at home a statue of Our Lady of Lourdes with the rosary in her hands and a photo of Padre Pio!

# 18. Jesus Breaks Evil Bonds

If you've been to a false 'healer' for yourself or for your child, go to a priest who knows of these dangers and ask Jesus' pardon for this practice. Also, ask the priest to pray so that every tie with darkness that has been woven between the deadly words of the healer and you (or your child), is severed. Often a good confession is enough to interrupt this evil chain. The sacrament of reconciliation is very powerful upon this type of evil. But it is necessary to renounce evil and close the door to every type of occult practice. You can also repeat the promises of your Baptism; it is very important to break off every type of bond with Satan, with his seductions and his works. Fasting, together with prayer, will truly heal us. The Lord gives us true healing, not that of false healers or surrogate healings which Satan and his servants propose to us (often by way of lots of money). The Lord truly heals, and not only our bodies, but also our hearts, our spirits and our souls. It is impossible to recall all the benefits of fasting, but I would like to list here some of the most important, knowing that the list is very long! To disarm demons or protect ourselves from evil is just one of the many fruits of fasting. And here are others equally valuable: obtaining physical, psychological or spiritual healing; free the souls suffering in Purgatory; create in our hearts extra space for the holy spirit and be thus more inspired by him; have a pure spirit; prevent and stop war (in ourselves, in our family, and in the whole world); suspends natural laws (tsunamis, avalanches, earthquakes or other natural catastrophes); creates a better understanding of God's plan for us and allows it to come to full fruition; we receive a great interior peace; we feel very free. Fasting reduces the length of purification in Purgatory, brings out our hidden dependencies quickly, and has the power to overcome them; improves our own health; enables us to fulfill our own inspiration, a song, buying a house, an icon…(the artisans of icons fast before beginning their work, this is the rule!); pours out the Blessing of God on marriage plans; obtains God's favor for you or others, for a conversion, a reconciliation, the return of a spouse or a prodigal child…

The list goes on. We are not talking about dreams; we are living it in Medjugorje.

# Frequently Asked Questions

## *What kind of bread?*

It is true that it is hard to fast with bread bought from the shops because it is full of preservatives and additives and un-enriched flour. And so, it is better to fast with a more enriched bread, made with whole wheat flour, from corn or barley cereals. For fasting days, try to find whole meal bread, something to calm your hunger. Our Mother doesn't want us to suffer from hunger on fasting days. As we all know by now, there are cereals and flours that contain wheat, and those that do not. Today we see a great many people who are allergic to gluten, often contained in wheat products such as wheat, rye, oats, barley and spelt. So out of these, we recommend using spelt flour which can be made into bread. Spelt has been the leading cereal to be cultivated in Europe for over 9,000 years. It is famous for having been the staple food of the roman Legions. In the 1800s it was also grown in the United states and Australia only later to be replaced by wheat, which gave a greater yield, was less susceptible to disease, and in general was more lucrative than spelt.

Today, spelt has made a resurgence in modern societies around the world beginning in the 1980s with the health/organic food industries. It can be found in the form of flour, pasta, noodles, semolina or whole beans. There are three types: small, medium and large; this last one is the most popular.

Not only is spelt high in protein (15-21%), it is also rich in iron, magnesium and amino acids, potassium and Vitamin B. For many, spelt substitutes well for wheat since it contains far less gluten than wheat. In addition, spelt does not irritate the intestinal mucosa in the lining of the stomach and is a powerful immunological stimulant. Saint Hildegard, considered it "the king of cereals." Of note, when spelt is cultivated, it does not need pesticides or other chemical substances, and the double husk protects it from radiation, especially nuclear.

If you are allergic to wheat or one of the rare people to be allergic to spelt, here is a list of cereals that make good substitutes: rice, corn, millet, quinoa, amaranth and buckwheat.

But be aware! Nutrition, which occupies an exaggerated place in the west, should not be at the center of our thoughts. If circumstances prevent us from finding the best suited bread, then let us be content with the bread we have, however poor, because God will compensate this want in his way, always Divine.

Some Saints, like the Curé of Ars, would eat very poorly, but he fasted with love, and the Lord filled in the rest. When Our Lady came in Medjugorje, families were very poor, and felt blessed each day that they had bread on the table with which to fast, it didn't matter what kind, and it is to them that the Blessed Mother has chosen to appear!

Our Lady has not said if the bread is to be toasted or not. For some people toasted bread is more easily digested. Then, why not? So, if you want to bake the bread at home, you can use the recipes available at the end of this book. When Our Lady speaks of water, she doesn't specify if the water should be hot or cold. You can play it by ear according to the temperature of the season. Another point of advice, even though it is a habit for many of us to automatically put ice in our drink, Father Slavko often said, and it has been corroborated by several doctors, that very cold beverages are to be avoided, while hot ones help with digestion.

## What are the best times of day to fast?

Here is a good question! The Virgin Mary tells us to fast on Wednesdays and Fridays. and we know the day starts at midnight and ends the following midnight. If, however, you need to do night shifts, it's possible to adapt the schedule. You can also tweak your own hours for fasting to accommodate your work schedule. Often, grandmothers tell me: "Wednesday is just the day in which I have my grandchildren with me at home, it wouldn't be a good day to fast!" In this case, it may be very well to move your fast day from Wednesday to Tuesday, the Madonna will neither look nor worry! When fasting day happens on a Feast Day, for example, if the annunciation falls on a Friday, one should not fast that day, but we can fast Saturday, Sunday, or the following Monday instead. You will understand, consciously, in prayer, how Our

Lady asks you to begin your fast. Sometimes in steps. For example, she has said of the rosary: "Don't impose the entire rosary on one who has never prayed it. May he/she today say an Our Father with the heart, tomorrow a Hail Mary with the heart, the next day a glory Be with the heart."

The same goes for fasting. if one can start at once on bread and water two days a week, great! Give thanks to the Lord! But you can also proceed in steps. It's better to begin little by little than abandon the effort, and not start too fast so that one doesn't stop after two months. You could start at lunch on Friday, then add lunch on Wednesday, then add dinner Friday, and go from there little by little. What's important, I repeat, is to fast with the heart. The Blessed Mother asks us to take on the firm decision to fast with the heart, in thanksgiving for her coming to Medjugorje, so that we do not have headaches or nausea. Vicka often says that if we are still troubled by these things, we have not yet made the decision to fast with the heart.

## *What about those who are sick?*

Our Lady says the sick are not required to fast, but that all those who are in good health are invited to fast. She asks the sick to offer their sufferings and make other renunciations.

For example, are you used to reading pornographic magazines and videos? Begin to give up this practice on Wednesdays and Fridays! Then renounce it the full week, because it is necessary to renounce sin. If you abuse your wife with your words, or by neglecting her, on these two days pay special attention to her, stop abusing her!

When one has a bad habit, we should start to renounce it on these two days and, little by little, sin will cease! Our Lady has said: *"Above all, dear children, I ask you to renounce the sin that dwells in you."* And also: *"Many come here to Medjugorje to ask God for a physical healing, but some live in sin. They don't realize they should seek first the health of the soul, which is the most important, and purify themselves. They should first confess and renounce sin. Then they can plead for healing"* (January 5, 1984).

> She added: *"Dear Children! I invite you to pray and fast for world peace. You have forgotten that with prayer and fasting it is possible to also avert war and even suspend natural laws. The best fast is that of bread and water. All, except the sick, should fast. Almsgiving and works of charity can't replace fasting,"* (July 21, 1982).

I suggest to those who are ill some form of renunciation, in addition to those cited by the Blessed Mother, such as alcohol, TV, surfing on electronic devices, tobacco, coffee. We would do well to renounce "junk food" from fast food restaurants. Our Mother doesn't want us to get sick. Our health is a gift that, as the others, must be preserved. If we could also give up gambling, electronic games, useless reading (fashion, cooking, comforts), listening to music, shopping, speaking negative words, complaining about your pains and sufferings of the moment, dressing provocatively. We could decide to spend less time on the internet too. I see people who don't realize the time they spend on video games (cell phones, tablets, PC's). You could stop consulting horoscopes, going to magicians, witches, fortune tellers or soothsayers of all kinds! We only think of the word "sacrifice," but we should offer to share our food with the poor, offer a book or DVD to a person who can't afford it, have a Mass celebrated for our adversary, or for the souls in Purgatory. We could eat those things we don't like, to mortify gluttony, call or write to a person who is suffering of loneliness, patiently listen to a person who annoys us, place a fresh flower for the Virgin Mary on a domestic altar or at church. Learn by heart a passage of the gospels or a Psalm. What about meditating on the seven sorrows of the Madonna, reciting a decade of the rosary for a priest, or reading the life of the Saints, (Padre Pio to his spiritual children, recommended at least half an hour a day of spiritual reading).

## How much bread?

Another important detail: The Virgin Mary has never specified how much bread we should eat. It is beautiful that her explanations are so simple; this way we feel more free. Of course, we shouldn't think: "since I'm fasting, I'll eat quite a lot of bread." Let us eat in moderation and God will help us. We make our choices with a free heart. I remember a conversation between Mirjana and an American woman. After she heard that we should fast two days a week, with bread and water, she opened her eyes wide in amazement and said to Mirjana: "When I get up in the morning will the Virgin Mary let me have a cup a coffee with a very little amount of sugar, just so that I can wake up?" Mirjana answered: "Yes, but hurry before the Blessed Mary gets up!"

I tell you this to show you the atmosphere of love that we have with Our Lady. she never forces us; we are like children with our own mother. Maybe our American friend, after a few years of fasting, was even able to offer Our Lady her coffee.

Our Blessed Mother gives us the means to have a greater love in our heart and to bear fruit; she gives us the means to grow in joy, peace and freedom. We must welcome fasting as a gift from heaven.

I will let you in on a secret: for seven years in Medjugorje, I wasn't able to fast because when I was young I suffered from some illnesses. I was then part of "the weak club." In my house at Medjugorje, two out of fifteen had this problem, and on the days when the others fasted, we ate. I didn't like this one bit and it didn't matter how many times I said to the Virgin Mary: "Do something!" it was no use. So one day I approached her in a more sentimental way and I said: "Dear Gospa, you make me travel the world in order to share your messages, but you see how I skim over fasting in comparison to the other points! I will not be a hypocrite. Since I don't fast, I will not give great speeches about this topic, I will not talk about what I don't know. I ask you for this grace." And since our Lady has often spoken of the wonderful fruits of fasting, I added: "Don't you want me to have these fruits?"

Shortly after that I met a Mexican friend who experienced a remarkable conversion in Medjugorje and went on to create a great apostolate of spreading Our Lady's messages through television in Mexico. While we exchanged stories of living this ministry, I asked him: "When you lack this or that for the apostolate, what do you do?" He answered: "Everything you need for your apostolate, whether it be money, health, material or spiritual things, either for you or for others, Our Lady will give it all to you "if" you do all that she says!" That "if" changed my life! I could feel my inner weakness to fasting, so I spoke to the Blessed Mother one on one and I said: "From tomorrow onwards I will do all that you say!" It was as if these words had given me the grace. I told Mary: "Tomorrow I will fast with bread and water, please give me this grace! You know I'm not the queen of courage, so I ask you for this sign: that all day tomorrow (a Friday) I will not be hungry and not even feel like eating." And she did! I fasted all day and at night I was still going strong. That's how I received the grace of fasting. We need to ask with fervor.

It's normal for those who are sick not to fast. But know that fasting also heals some diseases. Discuss with your doctor how you may partially fast. Obviously, you must not abruptly abandon your medical treatments or throw away your medications: that's dangerous. However, fasting one meal a week on bread and water won't jeopardize your health. I know a person who had a serious stomach illness so she never fasted.

One day in prayer, she felt that she should start fasting, and fasting healed her stomach! Every case is different, so caution should be taken by those who have serious illnesses.

## *Why bread?*

Often I'm asked: "Why bread and water?" Why not potatoes, lentils or rice? It is simple. As I said before, everything is connected to the eucharist, to the Bread of Life. Jesus didn't say: "I'm the rice of life." He said: "I'm the Bread of Life." That's why we eat bread on the days that we fast. Let's not forget that Jesus is at the center of all that the Virgin Mary asks of us. By fasting on bread and water we become more capable of welcoming the Bread of Life. Also we become more open to eternal Life, and we will be filled with the water of life, until we become like a river that will water the whole world. Our Lady said it herself: "Dear children! Today, I invite you to decide for God, because distance from God is the fruit of the lack of peace in your hearts. God is peace itself. Therefore, approach him through your personal prayer and then live peace in your hearts and in this way, peace will flow from your hearts like a river into the whole world. Do not talk about peace, but make peace" (February 25, 1991).

Let us remember that it was Jesus who chose bread, a staple food in the diet of his time, humble food, available to all and essential to all. He wants to become the most essential thing for our souls. Bread should remind us of the grain that falls to the ground that dies in order to bear fruit: it is the story of redemption.

Finally, bread also expresses the necessary cooperation between God, the creator of all that is good, who puts at the disposal of man the fruits of the earth, and man who, with his work, transforms those fruits, as we are reminded by the beautiful prayer of the offering during Mass:

> Oh Lord, accept our gifts in this mysterious encounter between our poverty and your greatness. We offer you the things you have given us, and you in exchange, give us yourself! Through Christ our Lord.

## *Why me?*

When you fast, do not look at your neighbor's plate. This is very important! If you do, you may find yourself judging your neighbor who doesn't fast. Then we would be no different than the Pharisees who asked Jesus why his disciples did not fast (Lk. 5: 33). Maybe those Pharisees, not only didn't fast with the heart, but disregarded the fact that it wasn't easy to follow Jesus night and day. Walking all over Palestine, under the sun and in bad weather announcing the good news, eating whatever, whenever they could (and not always their favorite dish) must have been very difficult. They didn't fast just two days a week!

Remember, judging always comes from the devil. We should act according to our conscience while respecting the freedom of others. Maybe your neighbor, although in good health, is not fasting. If you pray humbly for him, perhaps one day he will start fasting and God will grant him many graces, like the workers at the last hour (Mt 20, 1-16). This is what it means to be a Christian.

It is good to fast and hope that more and more people will do so, but more importantly we fast because we are responding to God's call through our Lady.

## Be the extended hands of God

Fasting is an act of mercy that helps our heart to grow. You will no longer simply fast for your child, your husband or pastor, but your heart will grow to the size of God's heart. Your heart is capable of containing God! He will lay all his divine desires in your human heart. When we fast, we allow God to expand the boundaries of our heart and reach the vast heavenly sky.

Through fasting and prayer God wants to pour his divine power into us, so that it may reach all those who are in need in the world, especially those who suffer. To fast is to take the hands of these brothers and sisters. Our outstretched hands will communicate light, and give the joy of living to those who walk in darkness. We will help them kneel and say: "Our Father, thank you for the gift of life, for rediscovering the joy of living." We will become God's extended hands to those who don't believe and walk in darkness.

"Dear children! Today I invite you in a special way to open yourselves to God the Creator and to become active. I invite you, little children, to see at this time who needs your spiritual or material help. By your example, little children, you will be the extended hands of God, which humanity is seeking," (February 25, 1997).

If we fast with our heart, out of love, then our fast is merciful. True fasting is one of the most beautiful acts of mercy, because while we are on earth, we don't know who we have helped. Do I offer my fast for the reconciliation of families so that Satan will no longer tear them apart? Perhaps many couples who were thinking of getting divorced in Australia, Singapore, Canada or South Africa, will instead reconcile thanks to my fast. Only in heaven will we know. Maybe in New York or San Francisco the youth who are tempted by homosexuality, drugs, theft or any other kind of perversion, will not commit suicide, and will convert thanks to my fast done with love for them. Even if my neighbor is cooking a steak, whose enticing smell comes inside my house, I will stay true to my commitment to fast on bread and water. If I fast for the sick, then maybe some of them instead of dying in torment will turn to God and say "yes" to his mercy.

We do not know the fruits of our fast while on earth. The fruits of almsgiving are more tangible: if I bring some homemade chocolate chip cookies to a little old lady, then I have the consolation of seeing her joy. When I visit the sick and do other good deeds, it feels very rewarding. The fast that we give our Lord goes into the treasure chest of the Mother of

God; she uses it as she wishes while to us it remains a mystery.

Maybe when we get to heaven, thousands of people will say to us: "One day even though the smell of steak and potatoes cooking was enticing, you stayed faithful to your fast and offered it for the unbelievers. Well that day, without you knowing it, while strolling along the streets of San Francisco the Holy Spirit touched me. I saw an icon of Christ in a store and I realized that he is my Savior, I found my faith, I was saved and now I'm in heaven." Then another will tell us something similar and then a third and a fourth.

Maybe our fast converted a doctor who had just graduated and wanted to become rich by performing many abortions. Our fast will allow the Holy Spirit to reveal to him the value and splendor of each human life! Our Lady will give him her maternal womb so that he accepts, welcomes, and blesses life thus rejecting any idea of abortion. Thanks to this conversion, thousands and thousands of children will not be killed in the womb of their mother. All this can occur by resisting the enticing smell of the steak, persevering in my fast, and praying for unbelievers.

Fasting on bread and water is a great act of mercy; however, it attracts even more merit when we do it in secret. The Virgin Mary says: "Do everything possible to ensure that no one knows that you are fasting." Obviously, if we live in a community or in a family we can't do it in secret, but if we work in an office, during our lunch hour we don't have to let people know that instead of going to the restaurant, we will be eating a piece of bread in our car. If we can, we should fast in secret. Our Lady always urges us to fast in humility. On February 10, 1984 the Virgin Mary told the prayer group: "Pray and fast! I desire humility from you. But you can become humble only through prayer and fasting."

Fasting on bread and water is truly a great act of mercy! Let us give thanks to our Lord for the gift of fasting. Some have taken such a liking to it that they say: "Dear Gospa, two days a week? You could have asked for more!"

## *See that you can do it?*

Our Blessed Mother calls all of us to fast. But maybe now that it's your turn, you hear that subtle inner voice saying: "I can't do it, I won't even try!" Would a mother ask her children to do the impossible, as if she doesn't know our difficulties? She is a true mother, and she guides her children to achieve their full potential.

Slowly, step by step she teaches us first to walk, then to talk. She doesn't want us to stop at the first steps, the first words. No! She wants us to receive all of the gifts from God.

Among the pilgrims who come to see me, there are some who tell me: "Dear sister Emmanuel, I tried but…then I stopped." To those I always answer: "Start again." Restart the journey with humility. This is the way to sanctity; it is not in never falling, but in starting again with humility. Often it is hard in the beginning, but over time fasting will become a lifestyle for a deeper intimacy with the Lord.

It may help to drink tea or soup instead of cold water. We can add olives, nuts, seeds and fruits to the bread. Another great help is to prepare the fasting food the night before. Your neighbor's coffee in the morning may distract you from your intention to fast, and you may even feel sad because there is no breakfast! On Tuesday and Thursday night, before we close our eyes, let us ask the Virgin Mary to help us; let us not feel glum about fasting, but instead think of the fruits and power that we put in our Mother's hands. She is there and she listens to us. If she sees that we ask fervently and with a sincere heart, she will not hesitate to surprise us tomorrow, and the Queen will distribute her gifts widely.

# Interview with Milona

*(Assistant to Father Slavko)*

*Sr. E:* Milona, you've been in Mejugorje for many years, since 1984, and you know that the message of fasting has often been on Our Lady's lips. You have worked closely with Fr. Slavko, who was the champion of fasting, to put it mildly. What can you tell us about the experience of fasting?

*Milona:* Fr. Slavko used to say that our Lady doesn't talk about theories. She takes her children by the hand and starts. She doesn't linger with a thousand explanations, she simply begins. Fr. Slavko says we have to do the same, we just have to start. If she says fast, then let's do it, if she says from your heart, we try, if she says bread and water, we try, and then everyone adapts according to his own capabilities, but the most important thing is that we do it with our heart. Fr. Slavko used to say that she is the memory of the Church, and knows everything from the beginning. He also said that, being a devout Jew, she fasted on Mondays and Thursdays, and then she changed it to Wednesdays and Fridays. Our Lady lived in the world before Our Lord came. She welcomed Him, she walked with Him and became a Christian, which means his disciple, and she stayed after His ascension with the apostles, even while they were fasting. Now, as she is the 'memory' of the Church, she asks us to resume fasting two days a week.

I remember during a trip to Ireland with Fr. Slavko, we listened to the old Gaelic language (old Irish), and the word 'Wednesday' there means "small fasting," Thursday means "day between fasting" and Friday means the "day of the big fasting." That's the translation of these three days in the Irish language. You can't imagine Fr. Slavko's joy: "You see? Mary, the memory of the Church." It was the time (a Marian year) when the Holy Father, John Paul II, had written the encyclical "Redemptoris Mater." It was that year that we found out all these things. And one of the titles given to our Lady was actually "Memory of the Church."

In the beginning, Fr. Slavko loved to say, the apostles used to fast before any decisions, for every choice they had to make. Fasting belongs to the Church from the very beginning. Fr. Slavko did some research and found that fasting has always been part of the life of the Church. He said it has been forgotten, and today we have just two small fast days: Good Friday and Ash Wednesday. He would laugh when he said that we have a wonderful way of fasting: eating fish. I come from Bavaria, where on Ash Wednesday we eat the best fish in the world. It's unbelievable, we finish the dances of Mardi gras and at midnight on the Tuesday night everyone is ready with the fish. Fr. Slavko used to say that fasting and prayer are like two lungs, or two feet for the spiritual life: it's a personal discovery for everyone.

I started fasting in 1984. Fasting with bread and water meant that I suffered from headaches and bad moods, and the same was happening to Fr. Slavko. He was smiling, saying "Well, if only those who fast have bad moods, then we wouldn't see that many people in a bad mood!" He used to say: fasting reveals what is inside of us, sometimes it reveals a disease, and this allows us to go to the doctor and find out what we are suffering from. It reveals things we would have never been aware of, as we have a way to console ourselves and to repress our disorders through food, chocolate...he himself was aware of these mechanisms, and used to tell us that when he started fasting, his first thought on Thursday night was: "Tomorrow there's no breakfast...tomorrow there's no breakfast!" It was really depressing. Then Friday morning came "no breakfast...no breakfast, no lunch, no dinner, an awful day." Then little by little he noticed that when he arrived full of joy to breakfast on Saturday...he wasn't hungry. What a delusion! All the desire to eat he had on Friday was gone by Saturday morning.

And, being an intelligent and knowledgeable person, he realized this was attributed to an addiction in the mind, psychological and physical. It's the habits, they cling onto us and we think that, without them, we are going to die. Step by step Fr. Slavko made this discovery with his life, as we make it ourselves on our own.

*Sr. E:* Tell us more about this discovery.

*Milona:* It's very simple, and by putting it into practice, it becomes clear. By doing it, we understand what it means. We can talk endlessly about fasting, but everyone will live it in a different way, as we do with prayer. I listened to Vicka who gave me some key points about fasting. She says, "the more you love, the easier it gets, it's all about opening the heart."

I remember once when I was fasting, it occurred to me to approach the Eucharist with much more joy and intensity than usual. I asked Fr. Slavko if this might be due to hunger, but he promptly explained it wasn't. In fact, my stomach was already full of bread. The eucharist had become alive for me, thanks to fasting I was hungry for the Bread of Life.

Often, hunger is more psychological than physical. Fasting is not a diet, as some people try to say, it is on a completely different level. We spoke to a doctor in France, Miriam Lejeune, she helped Fr. Slavko to prepare the weekly fasting retreats that started when the Balkan war broke out. She gave us some advice. For example: "Drink the bread and chew the water," which means do not gobble it down, but take your time, chewing slowly. You don't have to eat a kilo of bread; no, you have to eat slowly, with awareness, possibly in silence, so that peace will be created around you.

Miriam Lejeune created the retreat program: from Monday evening to Saturday morning, which meant four days of fasting: Tuesday, Wednesday, Thursday and Friday. At the arrival there was soup, on Friday evening soup again, and on Saturday morning a good healthy, tasty breakfast. It was an ideal situation, because everyone was fasting and was there for the same reason. We had an incredible "crisis" of laughter, especially with the nuns, because we could hear each other chewing. Suddenly, someone would start to giggle, and then everybody would burst into laughter and we couldn't stop ourselves. Some would drink tea with sugar, maybe putting only half a spoon in, just to survive mentally.

It is a tradition here in Bosnia to drink a strong delicious coffee; coffee breaks are a very important part of the day. One nun was concerned about the heavy migraines she would have if she did not drink coffee, because it's true it happens, I always had them. Then I said: "Look, try one day, try to take not even one of your pills." Now, one particular nun is completely healed from her migraines, she never gets them anymore. I don't know whether she drinks coffee now, but she is completely free from her migraines, and even more importantly, from the fear of them.

During the retreats, we could see tensions or specific pains lessen or even vanish from people. It's about relaxation, the body frees itself from stress in those moments. Anyway, fasting is not about "success" or reaching a "goal." Fr. Slavko used to say that you can fast all the time and completely miss the point, because the heart of the matter is to free oneself from sin, from egoism. The real goal is the fruit of fasting, which is fasting from sin, from egoism, from the attachment to ourselves and from always putting ourselves first.

Some days we feel the desire to fast, sometimes it's less intense, sometimes more, other days we must decide based on obedience alone. Sometimes we receive a great grace: we don't feel like fasting, but we pray for this and fasting becomes joyful. But there are also moments when one can't even stand to see bread!

Fr. Slavko often said: "How many people would like to eat the way we fast?". Many of them agreed: "Yes, this makes us aware of what bread means," because when you have no more bread you die, when you have bread you don't die. Of course, it's important to take care of your health. For example, when we started the fasting retreats, Professor Lejeune said that good bread has vitamin B, which is very healthy. So, she invited us to get bread made with a good recipe. It is better to have good bread which nourishes us enough rather than something that is just white and soft and makes us sick and suffer.

We can be intelligent about fasting, because it is not a false sacrifice. It is wrong to think that I need to punish or whip myself, it's not that at all. It's about a gift of love, an opening to love, to being "less egoistic." I would say this is the essence of fasting, the sense of the sacrifice we make. Sometimes, it is really tough to reach a clear understanding, we harbor fanaticism and self-conviction, but if we fast with humility, then a clear understanding will come. This is an important fruit, because we understand what is good for us. It helps us to discern and then everybody makes his own choices.

*Sr. E:* I like when you say that we must make a very strong decision. In fact, this decision is very important because, if you decide the night before to fast, it is easier than waking up the following morning and asking yourself "Should I fast today?" Then you start smelling the coffee and pastry of your neighbor and become sad because you have to fast. So, a firm decision is truly important. Our Lady is a very decisive woman, and she decides for love.

*Milona:* You know, I asked one of the visionaries what are the main differences she sees when she looks at Our Lady and when she looks at us, and she said: "She never said no to the Lord." The visionary added that we all say, at a certain point: "Ok, enough, this is too much for me." She didn't, she never said "no." From this comes her authority. The 'yes' she gave comes from total humility, from obedience, and from the freedom from herself. This is part of the behavior attributed to fasting, because fasting is, in fact, an inner disposition, not only something that we "do." Our Lady says we can change the laws of nature through fasting and prayer. Fasting and prayer are therefore very concrete things, which change things for real. We are at the peak of creation in this way, when we do something that brings us closer to our Creator.

He is with us, he creates anew, so he can change things through our "yes." Our Lady was a center of power, even as a child; her "yes" saved all mankind and made possible the coming of our Lord in this world through his own creation. If we follow her path and become her "yes," and she expects a joyful "yes" from us each moment of every day, then we will see great things happening in the future, for our life and for those around us. We want the world to change, we want it to become anew as she says, we need to be like Moses. Fr. Svetozar once said that we must leave behind ourselves many flowers as we walk the path of life, to plant, to sow, so that those who come after us can gather the harvest. It is a beautiful image, we really want to be people who follow Our Lady's path, so that others too may discover how beautiful it is, that it is worth following her, particularly our children and the future generations, because when we die we need to leave something good behind. This is already happening today.

*Sr. E:* I'm struck by the sobriety of her words. When we put together all the messages about fasting, there is almost nothing. She says it is best to fast with bread and water on Wednesdays and Fridays. People ask at what time should we start? Can we put butter on the bread? Should the bread be toasted or not? Should the water be cold or warm? Can we drink tea? She doesn't go into such details with us.

*Milona:* Sure, you can do it like that, bread and water. If someone puts butter on the bread, he will start to understand how wonderful butter is, like never before, because before, butter has always been under the jam. You can truly discover things in a new way. And how important water is, we have all these fruit juices and things like that, and all of a sudden you think "Wow, thank God for water!" You understand how wonderful water is.

When I went to Haiti after the earthquake, water had to be distilled and disinfected. we were in a shantytown, and there was no water. There was a tanker truck coming every day to bring fresh water, but we couldn't have it because it was exclusively for the people in the shantytown, so they gave us some warm Coca-Cola. I can't stand coke, and I can't stand it warm, but we needed something to drink to avoid dehydration. We had the opportunity to understand how important water really is, a person can die without water. We were by the sea, but we couldn't drink the sea water, because it's salty. Fresh, sweet water is such a grace, the living water. It's all connected, you know? The living bread, the living water. We could talk endlessly, if you think about it, there are many things to discover.

Fasting is simple, but it's a great universe to discover, which allows us to better understand the Bible, the Lord himself, who wanted to be bread for us. He said "Let anyone who is thirsty come to me and drink, he who believes in me..." (John 7: 37). He talks about bread, about eating and drinking, from the very beginning.

*Sr. E:* Yes, explain to us better this desire of Jesus to stay with us!

*Milona:* For sure, He revives me through the Eucharist, which is my only source of strength. The Eucharist gives me something more every time, it allows me to live His resurrection and to be with Him always. This is something wonderful and very regenerating. His resurrection is the most incredible thing that ever happened between heaven and earth. It was an unprecedented power! I always rediscover it, the fact that Jesus died and rose from the dead.

Fasting helps me with this, because it's something that goes beyond sentiments, beyond sensations, it is kind of bare. Bread and water are very sober, there are no-frills. There is no consolation, but through it God himself becomes the consolation. Young people can win against the spirit of the world this way because it sets you free. Over time through faithfulness to fasting you are not enslaved by the world anymore. It's not about power, it is his power, it is an enormous power but not how the world means it, it is very delicate: it is the power to forgive, to be able to suffer and to love.

*Sr. E:* When Jesus performed His first miracle, He took water to transform it into wine. It is not by chance, you know, He could have used something else.

*Milona:* What strikes me is that He made a truly delicious wine, not a cheap one, it was the best wine. This means that whatever He changes, He makes it into something marvelous, of great quality and beauty.

*Sr. E:* Remembering this miracle can help us mentally, when we drink our water, it is like we gave it to Jesus. We can repeat to Him, "Do what you please with this water I give you, but please do not forget to transform it into good wine, a special wine for those who most need it." Fasting is charitable, because it helps our brothers and sisters. This really touches me: with fasting it is possible to save souls.

Another great benefit of fasting is its revealing power. Yes, it is like an X-ray, or a CAT scan. One day we discover: "Oh,

I have this aggressiveness coming out," this means that something is not healed. Fasting reveals things which are hidden, you can stuff yourself with all kinds of earthly gratifications, and you forget that you are sick. But when all these gratifications are not available, the disease resurfaces and so then it can be cured.

*Milona:* Yes, all kinds of diseases can be revealed, both spiritual and physical.

*Sr. E:* That's right! When you have a tumor, you can live many years without knowing it; then by chance you have a CAT scan and it's discovered. What do you do? Do you get the tumor treated, or do you ignore it and resume your life as if it isn't there? For sure, you address the tumor and undergo all treatments needed. It's the same with fasting. It's a CAT scan which reveals the soul's disease. You can ignore it and keep it or you can cure it. For example, refusing to forgive for a wound that happened during childhood, a sexual abuse you kept secret until now, a sin you never confessed. Fasting, in fact, helps us to make a deep self-examination.

But what do you have to do? How do you get healed?

*Milona:* First of all, you must pray, go to Mass and go to Confession. Then...

*Sr. E:* But what about the human aspect, the hurt feelings?

*Milona:* It is a journey; everything is a journey. Feelings are one thing, but there is the 'will' and the decision to forgive. I don't always feel like it, but I decide. I want it, this is what is important. Feelings will be healed. I remember also Fr. Emiliano Tardif spoke about this, this amazing priest with a great healing gift.

*Sr. E:* Ah yes, he is going to be beatified!

*Milona:* He said that emotional healing takes time. Emotions are something different from 'will'. 'Will' matters, feelings are natural. Your power resides in your free will, whereas feelings come and go. Very often we don't forgive ourselves for our feelings. We think we should "feel" differently but we are unable to do it.

By accepting ourselves with our inadequacies, we can accept others with their inadequacies. It is not magic; it will take time. Then healing will happen. Feelings will resurface again and you think "Oh no, I thought I had made it." Bothering thoughts can come back, but you start again, then again…little by little.

*Sr. E:* There's some good in this: instead of giving God a gift a day, we give him a hundred!!

*Milona:* I remember that Br. Arcadius, a pilgrim priest, used to say: "Our Lady doesn't want a beautiful bouquet of flowers every day, she wants your little, withered flowers. She wants your daily failures, that's all she needs from you." This is all we have to give, it is very simple. St. Thérèse of Lisieux said "Jesus, be Thou my virtue."

*Sr. E:* It's a way to grow in humility, because when you see you are full of mess, wrong things, and that you are hungry for the virtue you don't have, you say "I can do nothing without you." In the end you get to rejoice for being so low, well, not low, but you know your capabilities, you are aware of your need for Him. On the other hand, if you feel great and you don't need Him, you are on the wrong path.

*Milona:* Yes, we depend on Him every day, on His resurrection!

# Testimonials

## *"If I had known...!"*

In my Community of the Beatitudes in Medjugorje, all of us can testify that Brother Jean-Michel had a problem with fasting, which I would qualify as instinctive.

But here is the story in Jean-Michel's own words: "There are two days in the year that frighten me:

Ash Wednesday and good Friday, because the Church asks us to fast on these days. I find it difficult to get into fasting. Within my Community, I am in the minority who eats full meals on fasting days. Yet, recently I found myself registering for the five-day "Fasting and Prayer" retreat held by the Franciscans in Medjugorje. I could feel that it was necessary for several reasons, but I harbored the secret hope that I would be told, "I'm sorry, the retreat is already full." Unfortunately, there was room for me.

As the retreat approached my anxiety grew and when D-Day came, I was completely terrified. It would have been enough for someone to tell me not to go. I would have gladly made an act of obedience; but no one relieved me. I was in such a panic that, upon the advice of a pilgrim, I went to pray at Fr. Slavko's grave and I begged him to come to my rescue, "You started this retreat, do something!"

On the first day of the retreat, I decided to let go of my fears and seize the grace of the present moment. I wanted to live each second, each planned event to the full, without any reserve. If I had thought that fasting would last for five days, I would have collapsed immediately. But the idea never went through my mind. It was the grace of all graces! Then I went to Apparition Hill and there I wrote a letter to the Blessed Mother. I explained to her all my worries and problems. I gave them all up to her so that I would no longer think about them during the retreat. I told her that I offered this week of prayer and fasting for her intentions and in exchange I asked her to take care of my problems.

To my great surprise, the retreat went amazingly well, without any difficulty. And when it ended, I was even able to go more deeply into the mysteries of the rosary by using the extra time offered on the retreat for meditation. I also found that I could live the Mass more intensely. I went into each part of it the way I would visit the different rooms of a beautiful castle, as our Franciscan priest had taught us.

I also give thanks for another unexpected gift I received on the fasting retreat. I had hydrocele, a hereditary disease of excess water in the genital parts, causing a frequent need to urinate. This handicap was a considerable inconvenience. Before going on a long trip or taking part in a time-consuming activity, I had to pay attention not to drink too much. At the beginning of the retreat, we were recommended to chew the bread well until it became liquid and to drink two or three big cups of herbal tea at each meal. Because I was very attentive to follow all prescriptions carefully in order to avoid headaches, nausea, or other problems, I never thought about the consequences that such a large quantity of liquid would have for me.

On the first day I drank a total of six big cups of herbal tea and nothing happened. At the time I did not pay any attention. The next day, I realized that I had gone to the bathroom only twice. Intrigued, I did the same thing again, and lo and behold everything was normal. I realized that I no longer had hydrocele. When the retreat ended, I quickly drank a glass of wine and a cup of coffee. The result is usually dramatic; but there it was, quite normal. Since that first day, I have not had any problems and I give thanks to the Lord for this unexpected healing. That's when I told myself, "If I had known, I would have made that retreat of fasting a long time ago!"

## *God defeats the insubordinate one*

Matthew, a very dear friend, has been a faithful pilgrim of Medjugorje since 1996. That year, after receiving a particular grace on Mount Krizevac, he experienced a conversion so deep that his life radically changed, much to the great joy of his wife, who had been praying, praying, praying for a very long time. He wholeheartedly embraced the principle messages of the Queen of Peace and began his education, doing his best to live out the well-known five stones in order to grow in the faith.[1] Maintaining his commitment to these objectives was something he couldn't guarantee after only five days in Medjugorje. He did that little by little.

Two years later, he no longer had any difficulty with monthly confession, the Eucharist, the daily reading of the Word of God, and the praying of the rosary.

But fasting, that preeminent endeavor among the five stones...impossible! There was nothing he could do. Every attempt on his part proved to be in vain, because he enjoyed gourmet food, was a connoisseur of the best wines of France, and enjoyed great health as well. Meal time, for Matthew, remained a sacred and incontrovertible necessity. Making things worse, he and his wife were excellent cooks, and their sense of hospitality often meant to them offering a bountiful table to their guests. When Matthew came to Medjugorje, he joked with his friends, "When you go to sister Emmanuel's house, if you want to eat well, avoid going there on Wednesdays or Fridays!" One day, Matthew asked me for advice: how could he finally succeed at fasting? Was he expecting me to reveal a quasi-magic remedy? Not really, because he had no actual hope of putting his problem to rest. He admitted to me that each time he took one step forward in his attempt at fasting, he had to take two steps back when it became obvious that it wasn't working for him. All the warning lights

---

[1] Praying the Rosary, fasting, reading the Bible, going to confession once a month, and receiving the Eucharist frequently.

from the Gospa in her messages on the necessity of fasting had become for him points of discomfort, of suffering, even of guilt. He enumerated for me a number of disastrous symptoms that attacked him when he began to fast.

"I tried forcing myself," he told me, "but to no avail. I would force myself to eat bread, but then I'd have a bad day. I'd be in a bad mood, and at 2 o'clock in the morning, when I couldn't sleep, I'd get up and go into the kitchen to have an omelette or something like that, so I could get back to sleep. Eventually, I gave up. Since I am retired from work in a city of pilgrimages, I organize with my wife my daily schedule, always putting Jesus first, since I don't have any more professional or family obligations (my children have started their own families). Each day: morning Mass and the rosary or Adoration in the early afternoon. But there's still the problem of fasting on Wednesdays and Fridays. I want bread to become my only nourishment two times a week, the way it is for the other apostles of the Gospa!

"You ought to try bread made with spelt," I told him. "That flour is really rich and contains all you need. It will really fill you up.[2] You can also use it in a bread machine.[3] And don't forget to give your struggle over to Jesus, from morning to night; you'll see. He'll help you!"

Matthew accepted the challenge. "I followed your advice," he wrote to me later. "The other day, after I had decided to buy a bread machine and spelt, I went to my local bakery to get some information on it and saw some loaves of spelt bread on the display shelf. It was a Tuesday, so I bought enough for the next day, Wednesday, but with no conviction that it would work. Wednesday morning, I cut into my new spelt bread with the firm resolution to eat only bread until the next morning. At morning Mass, I entrusted my fasting to Jesus, so he would help me. A miracle! The bread alone was enough. I fueled up all day on the bread: a marvel! I was

---

[2] Spelt is a rustic grain, the forerunner of wheat, which the Gaul (French tribe) consumed. Its cultivation goes back to 9,000 B.C. This cereal is famous for its nutritional and dietetic qualities. It contains the eight amino acids essential to the human body and improves the circulation of the blood. It is an exceptionally complete and very digestible food, ideal for fasting! The Bible mentions its use. (Ex.9: 32; Ez. 4: 9; Isaiah 28: 25). See the spelt recipe in its entirety on page 143.

[3] Bread machines allow you to make bread in 2 or 3 hours, depending on the machine. You put the ingredients in the machine and the bread comes out ready to eat. Those who fast can choose their flour and produce "homemade bread" without spending too much time at it. You cover the cost of the machine by saving your health, keeping in good spirits, and longevity!

amazed to have got past morning, noon, and night on spelt bread with some honey and water.

"The fasting hadn't been a trial. On the contrary, it was astonishing, because I hadn't suffered my usual upset stomach. I had a very good night, as though I had eaten normally at dinner, and woke up at 7 in the morning with no heaviness in my stomach. What's more, the entire day Thursday was spent in joy. I then committed myself to fasting on Wednesdays and Fridays for the intentions of our heavenly Mother. And to think it took me 17 years to find this recipe! Maybe it was a gift from St. Therese as well, because I had to live in Lisieux to find a bakery that made this bread. Fasting is no longer servitude but a source of joy that my wife shares with me."

Matthew was not afraid to leap into the water. All too often we want to understand a message from Mary or a verse from the Bible before putting it into practice. What a mistake! We miss so many graces that way! If heaven asks us to do something, what do we have to fear? Certainly, we have to organize ourselves in a way that allows us to live peacefully, looking for methods that are best adapted to our health, our families, etc. But it is only in living out the message that we discover the new horizons that are hidden behind it. There are secrets that don't reveal themselves until we act with confidence.

Fasting without love means you are just on a diet.

## Patrick, freed from alcohol and gambling

Lynda, from Scotland, shared a powerful event that occurred in her family, specifically with her brother Patrick, who was a slave to alcohol and gambling.

"My brother was the youngest in the family. Growing up he was a very good child. He was obedient and quiet but at the same time, full of fun. When he was 18, he went to college to train to be a medical doctor. He joined all the social groups and clubs that were available and partied with the best of them! He was really 'living it up.' He was drinking heavily and also got involved in gambling. "He qualified as a doctor and started working, but his career was not progressing. My family and I were very concerned about him and the amount of gambling he was doing. He had become seriously addicted. We tried talking to him, especially me in particular as I am his only sister and also his Godmother. I used to spend a lot of time visiting him at his apartment helping him to sort out his finances, manage his money and essentially get him back on the 'straight and narrow,' but unfortunately it wasn't working.

My mother was very worried about him and so we both decided to go to Medjugorje in October of 2012. We were walking to Fr Slavko's grave when my mother said to me "Look! There's sister Emmanuel over there, I want to go and ask her to pray for Patrick." She went over to her and asked her to pray. Sr Emmanuel responded by saying, "What does

Our Lady ask?" And my mother replied, "Prayer and fasting." Sr Emmanuel told her that in order to win such a war, she should do her whole part and not just half, she should pray and fast for her son and God would do the rest. Our Lady said, 'Through prayer and fasting, you can obtain everything!'

When my mother told me what Sr Emmanuel had said, my reaction was, "Thank God it wasn't me whom she said that to". However, when we returned home, as well as praying for my brother, we also started to fast on bread and water on Wednesdays and Fridays for him. Then we really saw a miracle happening.

That was two years ago and my brother completely stopped gambling. He is totally debt free! He has progressed a lot in his career, he's highly thought of as a doctor, and he has joined a team so that he can advance his career even further. Now he very rarely drinks alcohol. He may have a drink every now and again, but that is it. He's living a very good life, and has a lovely girlfriend. It was once we started to pray and fast that we really saw the miracle happening. Trying to talk to him before was like banging my head against a brick wall. Fasting had the power to break something within him that my family and I couldn't break through simple talking and prayer. Fasting was needed too. My brother grew up in a house of faith and love, but despite this, more was needed, and that was the power of both prayer and fasting." Lynda's testimony speaks to the hearts of many because the rate of addiction is massively increasing in today's world. Alcohol, drugs of all kinds, wrong sexual practices, gambling, etc are destroying so many families. If someone is not convinced by Jesus' words or Mary's messages about prayer and fasting, let him try it anyway; he has nothing to lose, but has a lot to gain!

## *Luca, a day of obedience*

"As a child I received a basic Christian formation, my mother being a Third order Franciscan. My father was atheist and completely absent. They separated when I was 15 and now, I am almost 40!

When I turned 18, I abandoned my family, my parish and my suffocating childhood and went to live in a southern Italian village, to "find myself," to work and try and obtain some sense to my existence.

For 18 long years I lived far from the faith and sacraments I had been brought up in. I plunged myself into work, amusement, and living a life of friendships and other things I was calling "love," but love it was not.

However, during this time in everything I did and experienced, a sombre shadow against life was constantly within me, which made me feel depressed, misunderstood and unhappy!

As time went by, I started noticing a sort of dark awareness in my heart. I did not want to live, I did not like to live, I couldn't stand myself and the war harboring in my heart had worn me down and defeated me…slowly all this showed itself in my hatred toward my family, my job, and the people

I was desperately clinging onto; those who were constantly betraying my love and thirst for Life.

Yes, I believe that I cohabited for too many years with a constant desire of not wanting to live...I got in touch with many new age disciplines, but thank God without ever practicing them properly: theta healing, rebirthing, channeling, Soka Gakkai, reiki, and many more such practices which have at their core the principles of spiritism, occultism and magic. I did not believe all that, but just from knowing about them and studying them a bit, the poisonous fumes of a dark evil got into my heart, telling me that the God I knew as a child and teenager was a fallacy, wrongly passed on by a deceiving and manipulating Church. So much so that a friend of mine, who was very much into some pseudo Buddhist philosophies, told me that Jesus did not die on the cross...what a great sorrow entered my mind, and then my heart when I heard those words.

I was not an example of a good Christian, but Jesus was to me the example of True love, who gives all of himself for those he loves.

*Brother Luca. Maria of the incarnation, Italy*

All of my work ventures in a short space of time failed, to the point that I found myself up to my eyes in debt, with poor health and unable to change my situation. The temptation of suicide had then become a very strong obsession; I remember spending hours thinking of a way to die without pain...I was no longer a person, but a human wreck at the mercy of despair. But...I remembered as a child, hearing about the apparitions of Our Lady in Medjugorje, and I recalled well that Our Lady was asking for the rosary to be prayed as well as fasting to obtain peace of heart. Peace of heart? Was that possible for me too?

I did some research on the internet, and in one of the many websites I found the suggestion of a book, written by a French nun, "Freed and healed through fasting," by Sr. Emmanuel Maillard. I found it straight away in a Catholic bookstore; I perfectly remember it was a Tuesday. I read the book in a few hours with great curiosity! I had a lot of time to plan my suicide, so I thought, why not in the meantime try to live a day of fasting on bread and water?

I saw it as a challenge, and my curiosity was pushing me to live "a different sort of day," even though feelings of anguish and sorrow were always in my head. The following day, Wednesday (Our Lady, in fact, asks us to fast on bread and water on Wednesdays and Fridays), I bought a nice piece of bread and decided that I would eat it when I felt hungry, and I would drink only water!

I do not recall the specific details of the day, however something strong entered in to me. From morning through to the evening I found myself with a completely light and free heart, my obsession with suicide had gone, and all the thoughts I had against life seemed ridiculous and stupid. I didn't pray or have any spiritual thought; I just told Mary that, if it didn't work, I would have to keep looking for a way to kill myself. Around evening time, before sunset, I left the house...the sky was the most beautiful and new thing I had ever seen. I didn't want to cry because I didn't want to disillusion myself and become disappointed...instead I started laughing to myself, thinking about suicide sounded so stupid that it made me laugh. My life had completely changed in only one day! All I did was obey Our Lady!

Fasting has an enormous spiritual power, like a torch shedding light on my inner darkness; it showed me all Satan's traps that were planted in my mind and in my heart. I understood that for years I hadn't been the one doing the thinking, but that the evil one was guiding my thoughts against life, against love, against joy and most of all against Jesus, Master and Lord!

Fasting and the holy rosary cause the immaculate heart to triumph, first within us and then all around us! The following day, a Thursday, I entered a Church and approached the confessional: I waited in line and, when my time came, I was embraced by the Father of all Mercy! This time, yes, I could cry all my tears of joy...the path has been beautiful and very hard at the same time: I had to let our Lady teach me a new Christian life...over time, the desire to consecrate myself to the Lord slowly matured. I am now consecrated, living a small inner monastic life, but, as I like to define myself, I am nothing; I am just a man who is "happily forgiven"! Some days I feel very tired, but by trying to stay little and obedient to Our Lady we receive the joy that doesn't come from the world (from worldly things) and we receive the graces and blessings to keep going with the confidence of being her "Dear Children."

Thank you, Mary, Queen of Peace, my Queen and my empress".

# What the Saints Tell Us . . .

## *The shepherds of Fatima*

"Francisco proposed a good sacrifice: "Let's give our food to the sheep so that we make the sacrifice of going without food." Within a few minutes, all our provisions were distributed to the flock. This is how we offered a morning of fasting, in a way that the most austere Carthusians had never done. It was not the only way we would fast. We also decided to give our food to the poor every time we met them, and those poor children so pleased to receive our alms, purposely waited on the street to meet us."

## *St. John Paul II*

"Here are some interpretations of fasting in our days: the renunciation of the senses, stimuli, pleasures, food and drink, the list goes on. It only has, as we say, to pave the way to profoundly contain, that from which the interior man 'is nourished.' This renunciation, this mortification, should serve to create in man the conditions to be able to live the higher values of which he, in his own way, 'is in need of'…It is now surely easier for us to understand why Our Lord Jesus

Christ and the Church call us to fast and do penance, i.e., through conversion. To convert to God, it is necessary to discover within us all that renders us sensitive to all that belongs to God, for example, the spiritual uplift, superior values, which speak to our intellect, our conscience, our 'heart' (according to Biblical language). To open oneself to the spiritual depths, to these values, it is necessary to detach from all that serves consumerism, and sensual pleasures. In opening our human personalities to God and fasting — both in the 'traditional' or 'modern' ways, it must go hand in hand with prayer because it directs itself to him. However, fasting, the mortification of the senses, the control of the body, gives prayer a greater effect, which man can find in himself. He finds, in fact, that it is 'different,' that it is greater than he can 'master by himself.' Then he becomes interiorly free. And, in conversion and the encounter with God, by way of prayer, fruit is borne within him.

In our reflections today, it is clear that fasting is not a 'by-product' of a religious practice of past centuries, but that it is indispensable to modern man, to the Christians of today."

## *Saint Faustina*

§ 531. November 24, 1935. On the first day, Sunday, I went immediately to the Blessed Sacrament and offered myself together with Jesus, who is in the Blessed Sacrament, to the Eternal Father. And I suddenly heard in my soul these words: "Your purpose and that of your companions is that of uniting to Me more closely, through "love." You will reconcile heaven and earth, you will soften the just anger of God, and will plead Mercy for the whole world. I commend to your care two precious pearls dear to My heart, which are the souls of priests and religious; for them you will pray in a particular way; the depth will depend on your annihilation. Prayers, fasting, mortifications, fatigue, and all suffering, shall unite you to My prayer, fasting, mortifications, fatigue, and sufferings, and now they shall have merit before My Father."

## Saint John Bosco:

### The dream of the 10 diamonds

"While I was sleeping, I found myself in a beautifully decorated large room. Suddenly there appeared a majestic man, who was so glorious that I hardly looked at him. He wore a majestic cloak, a rich mantle over his whole body. He had a sash knotted twice around his neck and a small ribbon was hung on his chest. On the sash in bright letters was written: The pious Society of Saint Francis of Sales in the year 1881, on the side of the sash was written: How it should be. Ten diamonds of extraordinary size and splendor were preventing me from gazing, without difficulty, on this great man.

Three of these diamonds were on his chest: on one was written faith, on the other, hope and on the third over his heart, charity. The fourth diamond on his right shoulder had work written on it, the fifth on his left shoulder read temperance.

*St. John Bosco, Founder of the Salesians
and The Daughters of Mary Auxiliatrix*

The other five diamonds adorned the rear part of the mantle and were arranged as follows: the largest and most dazzling one was in the center of a square and on it was written Obedience.

The first on the right read Vow of Poverty. The second further down read, Premium. On the upper left was written: Vow of Chastity. The splendor of this one radiated a very special light and it drew and held our attention like a magnet attracts metal.

On the second lower left was written: Fasting. All the rays from these four diamonds shone towards the diamond in the center. These diamonds had rays like small tongues of flame on which various texts were written. Faith carried the following maxims: "Put on the armor of faith to win over the wiles of the devil..."

On the rays of Hope was written "Hope in the Lord and not in men. Let your hearts always be fixed on where there is true happiness." On the rays of Charity: "Bear one another's burden if you wish to fulfill my law. Love and you will be loved, love your soul and the souls of others. Recite the Divine office with devotion. Celebrate Holy Mass attentively. Make loving visits to the holy of holies."

On the word Work: "Remedy for concupiscence; powerfully arm against all the temptations of the devil." On the word Temperance: "Take away the fuel and the fire will die out. Make a deal with your eyes, your appetite and your sleep, so that the enemies may not ravage your souls. Intemperance and chastity cannot go together." On the rays of Obedience: "Obedience is the foundation and perfection of holiness." On the rays of Poverty: "The kingdom of heaven is for the poor. Riches are thorns. Poverty is not practiced by words but by love and deeds. Poverty opens the gates of heaven." On the rays of Chastity: "All virtues come together with it. The pure in heart see the secrets of God and shall contemplate God himself." On the rays of Reward: "If the rich reward attracts you, do not be afraid of the many hardships. He who suffers with me rejoices with me. What we suffer on earth is momentary; my friends shall enjoy eternal happiness in heaven." On the rays of Fasting: It is the most powerful weapon against the snares of the Devil, and the custodian of all the virtues. With fasting you can defeat all sorts of demons."

## *Saint John Chrysostom*

The value of fasting consists not only in avoiding certain foods, but in renouncing all sinful attitudes, thoughts and desires. Whoever limits fasting simply to food is not taking advantage of the great value it contains. If you fast, let it show in your works!

If you see a brother in need, take pity on him. If you see a brother being praised, do not be jealous. In order for fasting to be true, it cannot involve only fasting with the mouth; you must also fast with your eyes, ears, feet, hands and your whole body; with all that is interior and exterior.

You fast with your hands when you keep them pure through selfless service to others. You fast with your feet when you are swift to love and serve. You fast with your eyes when you do not look at impure things, or when you do not scrutinize others in order to criticize them. Fast from all that puts your soul and your holiness at risk. It would be useless to deprive your body of food, but to feed your heart with sordid things, with impurity, with egoism, with rivalries or with comforts.

You fast from food, but you allow yourself to listen to many vain and worldly things. You should also fast with your ears. You should fast from listening to things that people say about your brothers and sisters, to lies about others, especially gossip, rumors or harsh words that harm people.

Besides fasting with your mouth, you must fast by not saying anything that could harm anyone else. after all, what good is it for you to abstain from meat if you devour your brother?

## Saint Peter Chrysologus

"Let ours be the fasting of simplicity...hidden to men, unknown to the Devil, known to God. Fasting washes the filth from the senses, cancels the sins of the soul, dissolves the faults of the heart, makes the stains from the heart itself disappear and leads with splendor the whole man to the candor of chastity."

There are three things, my brothers and sisters, by which faith stands firm, devotion remains constant, and virtue endures: they are prayer, fasting and mercy. Prayer knocks at the door, fasting obtains and mercy receives. Prayer, mercy and fasting: these three are one, and they give life to each other.

Fasting is the soul of prayer; mercy is the lifeblood of fasting. Let no one try to separate them; they cannot be separated. You must have all of them, for if you have only one, you have nothing. Let us use fasting to make up for what we have lost by despising others.

Let us offer our souls in sacrifice by means of fasting. There is no other offering more pleasing to God than this, as the psalmist prophesized: "A sacrifice acceptable to God is a broken spirit; God does not despise a broken and contrite heart." (Psalm 51: 17)

Offer your soul to God; make him an oblation of your fasting, so that your soul may be a pure offering, a holy sacrifice, a living victim, remaining your own but at the same time offered to God.

Whoever fails to give this to God will not be excused, for if you are to give him yourself you are never without the means of giving.

To make these acceptable, mercy must be included.

Fasting bears no fruit unless it is watered by mercy. Fasting dries up when mercy dries up. Mercy is to fasting what rain is to earth. However, much you may cultivate your heart, clear the soil of your nature, root out vices, sow virtues, if you do not release the springs of mercy, your fasting will bear no fruit.

## *Saint Alfonso Maria de Liguori*

He, who is attached to gluttony and doesn't practice mortification, will never achieve great spiritual heights.

## *Saint Leo the Great*

Fasting is the most pleasing prayer to God and frightens Satan. It enables us and others to be saved. Fasting is the most powerful means to get closer to God! Let us not neglect this powerful tool, this therapy which helps to heal our wounds. Value your good fortune: the one who receives much has to give much. Let the fast of believers become food for the poor.

## Saint Thomas Aquinas

When the devil is defeated in tempting you to gluttony then he will cease to tempt you to lust.

## Saint Augustine

"Fasting cleanses the soul, uplifts the mind, subjects one's flesh to the spirit, renders the heart contrite and humble, scatters the clouds of concupiscence, quenches the fire of lust, and kindles the true light of chastity. It brings you back to your own self anew."

## Saint Cure of Ars

". . . . The devil is not massively afraid of the discipline and other instruments of penance. That which defeats him is the curtailment of one's food, drink and sleep. There is nothing the devil fears more; consequently, nothing is more pleasing to God. Oh! How often have I experienced it!

Whilst I was alone — and I was alone for eight or nine years, and therefore quite free to do what I wanted, it happened at times that I refrained from food for entire days. On those occasions I obtained, both for myself and for others, whatsoever I asked of Almighty God."

"I bought from the poor the morsels of bread that were given to them; I spent a good part of the night in the church; there were not many people to confess like now...and God granted me extraordinary graces..."

"Every time that we deprive ourselves of anything which gives us pleasure, we are practicing a fast which is very pleasing to God because fasting does not consist solely of privations in eating and drinking, but of denying ourselves that which pleases our taste the most. Some mortify themselves in the way they dress; others in the visits they want to make to friends whom they like to see; others in the conversations and discussions which they enjoy. This constitutes an excellent fast and one which pleases God because it fights self-love and pride and one's reluctance to do things one does not enjoy or to be with people whose characters and ways of behaving are contrary to one's own..."

## *Saint Francis De Sales*

"Here is some advice. If you are able to fast, it would be good to fast not just on the days ordered by the Church, but a few more days. Besides the ordinary effect of fasting in freeing the spirit, subduing the flesh, practicing virtue, confirming goodness, and obtaining heavenly rewards, it is also a great tool to help us control our greediness, and to keep the sensual appetites and the whole body subjected to the spirit. Even if we don't fast often, the enemy will be more afraid of us when he realizes that we are capable of fasting.

## *Prayer for the night before fasting*

*Dear Jesus, you know that tomorrow is a day of fasting. You also know that I have decided to fast as your Mother strongly invites us to do. However, Jesus, to tell you the truth, I need you because you know how attached I am to food, and fasting is a renouncement that is always costly for me. O dear Jesus, stay close to me on this day, I beg you, do not allow my temptations to overtake and steal the grace that you have prepared for me. I'd love to help you reach those many hearts that are closed to your call today. I know that with my fast, you will be able to fill them with the light of your love. But you know how weak I am. Therefore, dear Jesus, I ask you for the grace to fast with all my heart, staying focused on the hidden fruits of conversion for my dear ones and so many others, without thinking of the food that I cannot eat.*

*Now, Jesus, together with you, I make my decision to fast. Be my strength, my God! With you all is possible and I'm not afraid!*

*What joy when I think of the millions of children that tomorrow, following the school of your Mother, will be with me spiritually, fasting on bread and water! I will not be alone, and this will fill me with joy. We are in fact the apostles of your Mother, the Queen of Peace, as she calls us, and I know how much she needs us to fulfill her plans for the world...What an honor to be a part of these children!*

*Well Jesus, the simple fact that I spoke with you gave me strength. Let us move forward together! I abandon myself to you with great confidence and I thank you for being with me always! I unite my fast to your fast in the desert, this way it will have great value and I rejoice immensely! Thank you, Jesus!*

# Messages of Our Lady on Fasting

## *1981*

June 26: "I am the Blessed Virgin Mary. Peace, peace, peace! Be reconciled! Only Peace! Make your peace with God and among yourselves. For that, it is necessary to believe, to pray, to fast, and to go to Confession".

November 16: "The devil is trying to conquer us. Do not permit him. Keep the faith, fast and pray. I will be with you at every step."

December 8: "...If you do not have the strength to fast on bread and water, you can give up a number of things. It would be good to give up television, because after seeing some programs, you are distracted and unable to pray. You can give up alcohol, cigarettes, and other pleasures. you yourselves know what you have to do."

## 1982

January 21: (The visionaries ask what to do to stop quarrels among priests) "Fast and pray".

July 21: "The best fast is on bread and water. Through fasting and prayer one can stop wars, one can suspend the laws of nature. Charity cannot replace fasting. Those who are not able to fast can sometimes replace it with prayer, charity and confession; but everyone except the sick must fast."

August 18: (to Mirjana) "Have the sick believe and pray; I cannot help him who does not pray and does not sacrifice. The sick, just like those who are in good health, must pray and fast for the sick. The more you believe firmly, the more you pray and fast for the same, the greater is the grace and mercy of God."

September 4: "...In the meantime, if you wish to give yourselves completely to God and if you wish that I be your protector, then confide to me all your intentions, your fasts, and your sacrifices so that I can dispose of them according to the will of God."

## 1983

August 29: (About a group of young people before a pilgrimage to a youth festival) "Convey the messages which I have given you. Do not hesitate to speak to them about it. Some begin to pray and to fast just as they have been told, but they get tired very quickly, and thus lose the graces which they have acquired."

October 29: (to Jelena) "You must strive to pray. Prayer is the only road which leads to peace. If you pray and fast you will obtain everything that you ask for."

November 8: (to Jelena) "Pray and fast! All that you can do for me is to pray and fast."

## 1984

January 19: (to Jelena) "Pray and fast, because without prayer, you cannot do anything".

January 27: (to Jelena) "Pray and fast. I wish that you always deepen your life in prayer. Every morning say the Prayer of Consecration to the heart of Mary. Do it in the family. Recite each morning the Angelus (once), the Lord's Prayer, the Hail Mary and the Glory Be five times in honor of the holy Passion, and a sixth time for our Holy Father the Pope. Then say the Creed and the Prayer to the holy spirit; and if possible, it would be well to pray one part of the rosary."

February 10: (to Jelena) "Pray and fast. I desire humility from you; but you can become humble only through prayer and fasting."

February 13: (to Jelena) "Pray and fast. Give me your hearts. I desire to change them completely. I desire for them to be pure."

February 26: (to Jelena) "Pray and fast. Know that I love you. I hold all of you on my knees."

March 1: Thursday, "May each one find his way to fast; he who smokes may abstain from smoking; he who drinks alcohol, have him not drink. Have each one give up something which is dear to him. May these recommendations be conveyed to the parish!"

March 5: (to Jelena) "Pray and fast! Ask the holy spirit to renew your souls, to renew the entire world."

March 14: "Pray and fast so that the kingdom of God may come among you. Let my son set you aglow with his fire."

April 24: "So many people, after they have begun to pray, to be converted, to fast and to do penance here, quickly forget when they return to their homes and to their bad habits."

May 30: (to Jelena) "The priests should also visit families, more particularly those who do not practice anymore, and who have forgotten God. Priests should carry the Gospel of Jesus to the people and teach them how to pray. And the priests themselves should pray more and also fast. They should give to the poor what they don't need.

## *1985*

September 26: (to Marija) "Dear children, I thank you for all the prayers. Thank you for all the sacrifices. I wish to tell you, dear children, to renew the messages which I am giving you. Especially live the fast, because by fasting you will achieve and cause me the joy of the whole plan, which God is planning here in Medjugorje, being fulfilled. Thank you for having responded to my call."

## *1986*

September 4: (to Marija) "Dear children, today again I am calling you to prayer and fasting. You know, dear children, that with your help I am able to accomplish everything and force Satan not to be seducing you to evil and to remove himself from this place. Dear children, Satan is lurking for each individual. Especially in everyday affairs, he wants to spread confusion among each one of you. Therefore, dear children, my call to you is that your day would be only prayer and complete surrender to God. Thank you for having responded to my call."

December 4: (to Marija) "Dear children, today I call you to prepare your hearts for these days when the Lord particularly desires to purify you from all the sins of your past. You, dear children, are not able by yourselves and therefore, I am here to help you. You pray, dear children! Only that way shall you be able to recognize all the evil that is in you and surrender it to the Lord so the Lord may completely purify your hearts. Therefore, dear children, pray without ceasing and prepare your hearts in penance and fasting. Thank you for having responded to my call.

## *1987*

January 28: (to Mirjana) "My dear children! I come to you in order to lead you to purity of soul and then to God. How have you listened to me? At the beginning, without believing and with fear and defiance toward these young people whom I have chosen, then afterwards, most of you listened to me in your heart and began to carry out my maternal requests. But that did not last for long. Whenever I come to you my son comes with me, but so does Satan. You permitted, without noticing, his influences on you and he drives you on. Sometimes you understand that something you have done is not agreeable to God, but quickly you no longer pay attention to it. Do not let that happen, my children. Wipe from my face the tears that I cry in seeing what you do. Wake up to yourselves. Take time to meet with God in the Church. Come to visit in your Father's house. Take the time to meet among yourselves for family prayer and implore the grace of God. Remember your deceased. Give them joy with the celebration of the Holy Mass. Do not look with scorn on those who beg you for a piece of bread. Do not turn them away from your full tables. Help them and God will also help you.

Perhaps it is in this way that God will hear you, and the blessing that he wants to give you in thanks will be realized. You have forgotten all this my children. Satan has influenced you also in this. Do not let that happen! Pray with me! Do not deceive yourselves into thinking 'I am good, but my brother next door is no good.' You would be wrong. I, your Mother, love you and it is for that reason that I am warning you about this. Concerning the secrets, my children, these are not known by the people. But when they will learn of them, it will be too late. Return to prayer! There is nothing more important! I would dearly wish that the Lord would permit me to enlighten you a little more on these secrets, but the grace which is offered to you is already great enough. Think how much you have offended him. What are you offering to him of yourself? When was the last time you renounced something for the Lord? I no longer wish to reprimand you in this way, but I want to invite you once more to prayer, to fasting and penance. If you wish to obtain a grace from God by fasting, then let no one know that you are fasting. If you wish to receive a grace from God by a gift to the poor, let no one know except you and the Lord that you have given this gift. Listen to me, my children! Meditate on my message in prayer."

## *1989*

14 January: "Dear children, I invite you to renew your fasting of all the senses: taste, sight, smell and tongue. Do

mortifications. In this way you will renew the prayer of your body. And beware that Satan in this time seeks to destroy all that you have obtained during Christmas time and the other feasts."

## 1991

July 25: (to Marija) "Dear Children! Today I invite you to pray for peace. At this time peace is being threatened in a special way, and I am seeking from you to renew fasting and prayer in your families. Dear children, I desire you to grasp the seriousness of the situation and that much of what will happen depends on your prayers and you are praying a little bit. Dear children, I am with you and I am inviting you to begin to pray and fast seriously as in the first days of my coming. Thank you for having responded to my call."

August 25: (to Marija) "Dear Children…Satan is strong and wants to sweep away my plans of peace and joy and make you think that my son is not strong in his decisions. Therefore, I call all of you, dear children, to pray and fast still more firmly…"

## 1992

March 25: (to Marija) "Dear children! Today as never before I invite you to live my messages and to put them into practice in your life. I have come to you to help you and, therefore, I invite you to change your life because you have taken a path of misery, a path of ruin. When I told you: convert, pray, fast, be reconciled, you took these messages superficially. You started to live them and then you stopped, because it was difficult for you. No, dear children, when something is good, you have to persevere in the good and not think: God does not see me, he is not listening, he is not helping. And so you have gone away from God and from me because of your miserable interest. I wanted to create of you an oasis of peace, love and goodness. God wanted you, with your love and with his help, to do miracles and, thus, give an example. Therefore, here is what I say to you: Satan is playing with you and with your souls and I cannot help you because you are far away from my heart. Therefore, pray, live my messages and then you will see the miracles of God's love in your everyday life. Thank you for having responded to my call."

April 25: (to Marija) "Dear children! Today also I invite you to prayer. Only by prayer and fasting can war be stopped. Therefore, my dear little children, pray and by your life give witness that you are mine and that you belong to me, because Satan wishes in these turbulent days to seduce as many souls as possible. Therefore, I invite you to decide for God and he will protect you and show you what you should do and which path to take. I invite all those who have said "yes" to me to renew their consecration to my Son, Jesus, and to His heart and to me so we can take you more intensely as instruments of peace in this unpeaceful world. Medjugorje is a sign to all of you and a call to pray and live the days of grace that

God is giving you. Therefore, dear children, accept the call to prayer with seriousness. I am with you and your suffering is also mine. Thank you for having responded to my call."

## *1999*

April 25: (to Marija) "Dear children! Also, today I call you to prayer. Little children be joyful carriers of peace and love in this peaceless world. By fasting and prayer, witness that you are mine and that you live my messages..."

## *2000*

June 25: (to Ivanka) "I introduced myself as 'Queen of Peace.' Again I call you to peace, fasting, prayer. Renew family prayer and receive my blessing."

October 25: (to Marija) "Dear children! Today I desire to open my motherly heart to you and to call you all to pray for my intentions. I desire to renew prayer with you and to call you to fast which I desire to offer to my Son Jesus for the coming of a new time — a time of spring. In this Jubilee year many hearts have opened to me and the Church is being renewed in the spirit. I rejoice with you and I thank God for this gift; and you, little children, I call to pray, pray, pray — until prayer becomes a joy for you. Thank you for having responded to my call.

## 2001

January 25: (to Marija) "Dear children! Today I call you to renew prayer and fasting with even greater enthusiasm until prayer becomes a joy for you. Little children, the one who prays is not afraid of the future and the one who fasts is not afraid of evil. Once again, I repeat to you: only through prayer and fasting also wars can be stopped — wars of your unbelief and fear for the future. I am with you and am teaching you little children: your peace and hope are in God. That is why draw closer to God and put him in the first place in your life. Thank you for having responded to my call."

September 25: (to Marija) "Dear children! Also, today I call you to prayer, especially today when Satan wants war and hatred. I call you anew, little children: pray and fast that God may give you peace. Witness peace to every heart and be carriers of peace in this world without peace. I am with you and intercede before God for each of you. And you do not be afraid because the one who prays is not afraid of evil and has no hatred in the heart. Thank you for having responded to my call."

## 2003

February 25: (to Marija) "Dear children! Also today I call you to pray and fast for peace. As I have already said and now repeat to you, little children, only with prayer and fasting can wars also be stopped. Peace is a precious gift from God. Seek, pray and you will receive it..."

## *2004*

July 25: (to Marija) "Dear children! I call you anew: be open to my messages. I desire, little children, to draw you all closer to my son Jesus; therefore, you pray and fast. Especially I call you to pray for my intentions, so that I can present you to my son Jesus; for him to transform and open your hearts to love. When you will have love in the heart, peace will rule in you. Thank you for having responded to my call."

## *2005*

March 18 (to Mirjana) "Dear children! I come to you as the mother who, above all, loves her children. My children, I desire to teach you to love also. I pray for this. I pray that you will recognize my son in each of your neighbors. The way to my Son, who is true peace and love, passes through the love for all neighbors. My children, pray and fast for your heart to be open for this my intention."

July 25: (to Marija) "Dear children! Also, today, I call you to fill your day with short and ardent prayers. When you pray, your heart is open, and God loves you with a special love and gives you special graces. Therefore, make good use of this time of grace and devote it to God more than ever up to now. Do novenas of fasting and renunciation so that Satan be far from you and grace be around you. I am near you and intercede before God for each of you. Thank you for having responded to my call."

## 2006

January 2: (to Mirjana) "Dear children, my Son is born. Your Savior is here with you. What prevents your hearts from receiving him? What is false within them? Purify them by fasting and prayer. Recognize and receive my Son. He alone gives you true peace and true love. The way to eternal life is he my Son! Thank you."

March 18: (to Mirjana) "Dear children! In this Lenten time, I call you to interior renunciation. The way to this leads you through love, fasting, prayer and good works. Only with total interior renunciation will you recognize God's love and the signs of the time in which you live. You will be witnesses of these signs and will begin to speak about them. I desire to bring you to this. Thank you for having responded to me."

October 2: (to Mirjana) "Dear children! I am coming to you in this your time, to direct the call to eternity to you. This is the call of love. I call you to love because only through love will you come to know the love of God. Many think that they have faith in God and that they know his laws. They try to live according to them, but they do not do what is the most important; they do not love him. My children, pray and fast. This is the way which will help you to open yourselves and to love. Only through the love of God is eternity gained. I am with you. I will lead you with the Motherly love. Thank you for having responded."

December 2: (to Mirjana) "Dear children, in this joyful time of expectation of my son, I desire that all the days of your earthly life may be a joyful expectation of my Son. I am calling you to holiness. I call you to be my apostles of holiness so that, through you, the Good News may illuminate all those whom you will meet. Fast and pray and I will be with you. Thank you!"

## *2007*

January 2: (to Mirjana) "Dear children, in this holy time full of God's graces, and his love which sends me to you, I implore you not to be with a heart of stone. May fasting and prayer be your weapon for drawing closer to and coming to know Jesus, my Son. Follow me and my luminous example. I will help you. I am with you. Thank you."

March 2: (to Mirjana) "Dear children, my name is Love. That I am among you for so much of your time is love, because the great Love sends me. I am asking the same of you. I am asking for love in your families. I am asking that you recognize love in your brother. Only in this way, through love will you see the face of the greatest Love. May fasting and prayer be your guiding star! Open your hearts to love, namely salvation. Thank you."

March 18: (to Mirjana) "Dear children! I come to you as a Mother with gifts. I come with love and mercy. Dear children, mine is a big heart. In it, I desire all of your hearts, purified by fasting and prayer. I desire that, through love, our hearts may triumph together. I desire that through that triumph you may see the real Truth, the real way and the real Life. I desire that you may see my Son. Thank you."

March 25: (to Marija) "Dear children! I desire to thank you from my heart for your Lenten renunciations. I desire to inspire you to continue to live fasting with an open heart. By fasting and renunciation, little children, you will be stronger in faith. In God you will find true peace through daily prayer. I am with you and I am not tired. I desire to take you all with me to heaven, therefore, decide daily for holiness. Thank you for having responded to my call."

September 2: (to Mirjana) "Dear children, in this time of God's signs, do not be afraid because I am with you. The great love of God sends me to lead you to salvation. Give me your simple hearts purified by fasting and prayer. Only in the simplicity of your hearts is your salvation. I will be with you and will lead you. Thank you."

November 2: (to Mirjana) "Dear children...My children, God is the immeasurable good and therefore, as a Mother, I implore you to pray, pray, pray, fast and hope that it is possible to attain that good, because love is born of that good. The Holy Spirit will reinforce that 'good' in you and you will be able to call God your Father..."

## 2008

January 2: (to Mirjana) "Dear children! With all the strength of my heart I love you and give myself to you. As a mother fights for her children, I pray for you and I fight for you. I ask you not to be afraid to open yourselves, so as to be able to love with the heart and give yourselves to others. The more you do this with the heart, the more you will receive and the better you will understand my Son and His gift to you. May everyone recognize you through the love of my Son and through me. Thank you!"

January 25: (to Marija) "Dear children! With the time of Lent, you are approaching a time of grace. Your heart is like ploughed soil and it is ready to receive the fruit which will grow into what is good. You, little children, are free to choose good or evil. Therefore, I call you to pray and fast. Plant joy and the fruit of joy will grow in your hearts for your good, and others will see it and receive it through your life. Renounce sin and choose eternal life. I am with you and intercede for you before my Son. Thank you for having responded to my call."

## 2009

March 18: (to Mirjana) "Dear children! Today I call you to look into your hearts sincerely and for a long time. What will you see in them? Where is my son in them and where is the desire to follow me to Him? My children, may this time of renunciation be a time when you will ask yourself: 'What does my God desire of me personally? What am I to do?' Pray, fast and have a heart full of mercy. Do not forget your shepherds. Pray that they may not get lost, that they may remain in my Son so as to be good shepherds to their flock."

Our Lady looked at all those present and added: "Again I say to you, if you knew how much I love you, you would cry with happiness. Thank you."

October 25: (to Marija) "Dear children! Also, today I bring you my blessing, I bless you all and I call you to grow on this way, which God has begun through me for your salvation. Pray, fast and joyfully witness your faith, little children, and may your heart always be filled with prayer. Thank you for having responded to my call."

## 2010

June 2: (to Mirjana) "Dear Children, today I call you with prayer and fasting to clear the path in which my Son will enter into your hearts. Accept me as a mother and a messenger of God's love and his desire for your salvation. Free yourself of everything from the past which burdens you, that gives you a sense of guilt, that which previously led you astray in error and darkness. Accept the light. Be born anew in the righteousness of my Son. Thank you."

## 2011

January 2: (to Mirjana) "Dear children, today I call you to unity in Jesus, my Son. My motherly heart prays that you may comprehend that you are God's family. Through the spiritual freedom of will, which the Heavenly Father has given you, you are called to become cognizant (to come to the knowledge) of the truth, the good or the evil. May prayer and fasting open your hearts and help you to discover the Heavenly Father through my Son. In discovering the Father, your life will be directed to the carrying out of God's will and the realization of God's family, in the way that my Son desires. I will not leave you alone on this path. Thank you."

March 2: (to Mirjana) "Dear children, my motherly heart suffers tremendously as I look at my children who persistently put what is human before what is of God; at my children who, despite everything that surrounds them and despite all the signs that are sent to them, think that they can walk without my Son. They cannot! They are walking to eternal perdition. That is why I am gathering you, who are ready to open your heart to me, you who are ready to be apostles of my love, to help me; so that by living God's love you may be an example to those who do not know it. May fasting and prayer give you strength in that and I bless you with my motherly blessing in the name of the Father and of the Son and of the Holy Spirit. Thank you."

August 25: (to Marija) "Dear children! Today I call you to pray and fast for my intentions, because Satan wants to destroy my plan. Here I began with this parish and invited the entire world. Many have responded, but there is an enormous number of those who do not want to hear or accept my call. Therefore, you who have said 'yes,' be strong and resolute. Thank you for having responded to my call."

## *2012*

March 18: (to Mirjana) "Dear children! I am coming among you because I desire to be your mother, your intercessor. I desire to be the bond between you and the Heavenly Father your mediatrix. I desire to take you by the hand and to walk with you in the battle against the impure spirit. My children, consecrate yourselves to me completely. I will take your lives into my motherly hands and I will teach them peace and love, and then I will give them over to my Son. I am asking of you to pray and fast because only in this way will you know how to witness my Son in the right way through my motherly heart. Pray for your shepherds that, united in my

Son, they can always joyfully proclaim the Word of God. Thank you."

June 2: (to Mirjana) "...My children, great is the responsibility upon you. I desire that by your example you help sinners regain their sight, enrich their poor souls and bring them back into my embrace. Therefore, pray, pray, fast and confess regularly. If receiving my Son in the Eucharist is the center of your life then do not be afraid, you can do everything. I am with you. Every day I pray for the shepherds and I expect the same of you. Because, my children, without their guidance and strengthening through their blessing, you cannot do it. Thank you."

October 25: (to Marija) "Dear children! Today I call you to pray for my intentions. Renew fasting and prayer because Satan is cunning and attracts many hearts to sin and perdition. I call you, little children, to holiness and to live in grace. Adore my Son so that He may fill you with His peace and love for which you yearn. Thank you for having responded to my call."

November 2: (to Mirjana) "...My children, great grace has been given to you to be witnesses of God's love. Do not take the given responsibility lightly. Do not sadden my motherly heart. As a mother I desire to rely on my children, on my apostles. Through fasting and prayer, you are opening the way for me to pray to my Son for Him to be beside you and for His Name to be holy through you. Pray for the shepherds because none of this would be possible without them. Thank you."

## 2013

January 2: (to Mirjana) "...My children, do not be afraid to open your hearts to me. I will give them to my Son and in return, He will give you the gift of Divine peace. You will carry it to all those whom you meet, you will witness God's love with your life, and you will give the gift of my Son through yourselves. Through reconciliation, fasting and prayer, I will lead you. Immeasurable is my love. Do not be afraid..."

March 2: (to Mirjana) "Dear children! Anew, in a motherly way, I am calling you not to be of a hard heart. Do not shut your eyes to the warnings which the Heavenly Father sends to you out of love. Do you love him above all else? Do you repent for having often forgotten that the Heavenly Father, out of his great love, sent his Son to redeem us by the Cross? Do you repent for not yet having accepted the message? My children, do not resist the love of my Son. Do not resist hope and peace. Along with your prayer and fasting, by His cross, my Son will cast away the darkness that wants to surround you and come to rule over you. He will give you the strength for a new life. Living it according to my Son, you will be a blessing and a hope to all those sinners who wander in the darkness of sin. My children, keep vigil. I, as a mother, am keeping vigil with you. I am especially praying and watching over those whom my Son called to be light-bearers and carriers of hope for you, for your shepherds. Thank you."

May 2: (to Mirjana) "Dear children, anew, I am calling you to love and not to judge. My Son, according to the will of the Heavenly Father, was among you to show you the way of salvation, to save you and not to judge you. If you desire to follow my Son, you will not judge but love like your Heavenly Father loves you. And when it is the most difficult for you, when you are falling under the weight of the cross do not despair, do not judge, instead remember that you are loved and praise the Heavenly Father because of his love. My children, do not deviate from the way on which I am leading you. Do not recklessly walk into perdition. May prayer and fasting strengthen you so that you can live as the Heavenly Father would desire; that you may be my apostles of faith and love; that your life may bless those whom you meet; that you may be one with the Heavenly Father and my Son . . ."

June 2: (to Mirjana) "Dear children, in this restless time, anew I am calling you to set out after my Son to follow Him. I know of the pain, suffering and difficulties, but in my Son you will find rest; in Him you will find peace and salvation. My children, do not forget that my Son redeemed you by His Cross and enabled you, anew, to be children of God; to be able to, anew, call the Heavenly Father: "Father." To be worthy of the Father, love and forgive, because your Father is love and forgiveness. Pray and fast, because that is the way to your purification, it is the way of coming to know and becoming cognizant of the Heavenly Father. When you become cognizant of the Father, you will comprehend that he is all you need . . ."

July 2: (to Mirjana) "Dear children, with a motherly love I am imploring you to give me the gift of your hearts, so I can present them to my Son and free you — free you from all the evil enslaving and distancing you all the more from the only good — my Son — from everything which is leading you on the wrong way and is taking peace away from you. I desire to lead you to the freedom of the promise of my Son, because I desire for God's will to be fulfilled completely here; and that through reconciliation with the Heavenly Father, through fasting and prayer, apostles of God's love may be born — apostles who will freely, and with love, spread the love of God to all my children — apostles who will spread the love of the trust in the Heavenly Father and who will keep opening the gates of heaven..."

September 2: (to Mirjana) "Dear children, I love you all. All of you, all of my children, all of you are in my heart. All of you have my motherly love, and I desire to lead all of you to come to know God's joy. This is why I am calling you. I need humble apostles who, with an open heart, will accept the Word of God and help others to comprehend the meaning of their life alongside God's word. To be able to do this my children, through prayer and fasting, you must learn to listen with the heart and to learn to keep submitting yourselves.

You must learn to keep rejecting everything that distances you from God's Word and to yearn only for that which draws you closer to it. Do not be afraid. I am here. You are not alone..."

December 2: (to Mirjana) "Dear children, with a motherly love and a motherly patience I am looking at your ceaseless wandering and how lost you are. That is why I am with you. I desire to help you to first find and come to know yourself, so that, then, you would be able to recognize and to admit everything that does not permit you to get to know the love of the Heavenly Father, honestly and wholeheartedly. My children, the Father comes to be known through the Cross. Therefore, do not reject the Cross. Strive to comprehend and accept it with my help. When you will be able to accept the Cross you will also understand the love of the Heavenly Father; you will walk with my Son and with me; you will differ from those who have not come to know the love of the Heavenly Father, those who listen to Him but do not understand Him, those who do not walk with Him who have not come to know Him. I desire for you to come to know the truth of my Son and to be my apostles; that, as children of God, you may rise above the human way of thinking and always, and in everything, seek God's way of thinking, anew. My children, pray and fast that you may be able to recognize all of this which I am seeking of you. Pray for your shepherds and long to come to know the love of your Heavenly Father, in union with them. Thank you."

## 2014

February 2: (to Mirjana) "Dear children...I desire that by fasting and prayer you obtain from the Heavenly Father the cognition of what is natural and holy — Divine. Filled with cognition, under the shelter of my Son and myself, you will be my apostles who will know how to spread the Word of God to all those who do not know of it; and you will know how to overcome obstacles that will stand in your way. My children, by means of a blessing, God's grace will descend upon you and you will be able to retain it through fasting, prayer, purification and reconciliation. You will have the efficiency which I seek of you..."

April 2: (to Mirjana) "Dear children, with a motherly love I desire to help you with your life of prayer and penance to be a sincere attempt at drawing closer to my Son and His Divine light that you may know how to separate yourselves from sin. Every prayer, every Mass and every fasting is an attempt at drawing closer to my Son, a reminder of His glory and a refuge from sin; it is a way to a renewed union of the good Father and his children..."

August 2: (to Mirjana) "Dear children, the reason that I am with you, my mission, is to help you for 'good' to win, even though this does not seem possible to you now. I know that you do not understand many things as I also did not understand everything, everything that my Son explained to me while He was growing up alongside me but I believed Him and followed Him. I ask this of you also, to believe me and to follow me. However, my children, to follow me means to love my Son above everything, to love Him in every person without making differences. For you to be able to do this, I call you anew to renunciation, prayer and fasting. I am calling you for the Eucharist to be the life of your soul. I am calling you to be my apostles of light who will spread love and mercy through the world. My children, your life is only a blink in contrast to eternal life. And when you come before my Son, in your hearts he will see how much love you had. In order to spread love in the right way, I am asking my Son, through love, to grant you unity through him, unity among you, unity between you and your shepherds..."

December 2: (to Mirjana) "Dear children, remember – for I am telling you — that love will win. I know that many of you are losing hope because around you, you see suffering, pain, jealousy, envy...but, I am your mother. I am in the Kingdom but am also here with you. My Son is sending me anew to help you. Therefore, do not lose hope; instead, follow me — because the victory of my heart is in the name of God. My beloved Son is thinking of you as He has always thought of you. Believe Him and live Him. He is the life of the world. My children, to live my Son means to live the Gospel. This is not easy. This means love, forgiveness and sacrifice. This purifies and it opens the Kingdom. Sincere prayer, which is not only words but is a prayer which the heart speaks, will help you. Likewise fasting (will help you), because it is still more of love, forgiveness and sacrifice. Therefore, do not lose hope but follow me..."

## 2015

January 2: (to Mirjana) "Dear children, I am here among you as a mother who desires to help you to come to know the truth. While I lived your life on earth I had knowledge of the truth, and by this alone, a piece of heaven on earth. That is why I desire the same for you, my children. The Heavenly Father desires pure hearts filled with the knowledge of the truth. He desires for you to love all those whom you meet, because I also love my Son in all of you. This is the beginning of coming to know the truth. Many false truths are being offered to you. You will overcome them with a heart cleansed by fasting, prayer, penance and the Gospel. This is the only truth and it is the truth which my Son left you. You do not need to examine it much. What is asked of you, as I also have done, is to love and to give..."

> * Messages of Our Lady referenced from 1981 2010 from "Words from Heaven" Revised 15th edition, published 2015 by Caritas of Birmingham, Sterrett, Alabama USA.

> * Messages of Our Lady referenced from 1985 2016 from www.medjugorje.org

# Recipes

## Fasting Bread

*3 cups white flour*

*4 cups wheat flour*

*1 pkg. dry yeast or three tablespoons of active yeast*

*½ cup of lukewarm water*

*2 cups of very hot water*

*1 beaten egg*

*1 Tablespoon of salt*

*2 Tablespoons of sugar*

*2 Tablespoons of olive oil*

*1 teaspoon of butter*

Depending upon your taste, you may add any of the following to the dough: raisins, fresh apple pieces, almonds, walnuts, plain oats.

Dissolve yeast in ½ cup lukewarm water with a little sugar and let sit in warm place for 5-10 minutes. Mix flour in a large bowl. Make a well in the middle of the flour. When yeast is ready, add to flour. Mix flour over yeast mixture making soft balls. In 2 cups of hot water, mix butter, oil, salt, sugar, raisins (or apple), nuts, and ½ beaten egg. Pour over yeast. Knead the dough until it comes clean from the bowl (continually add flour and water as needed). Let it rise 10 minutes, covered. Knead again until it is has spring to it. Place in well-greased bowl in a warm oven (70-80°F) until it is double in bulk. Form into desired shapes. Brush the top with remaining egg and sesame seeds, oats, or poppy seeds, if desired. Bake at 375°F for 35 minutes, until golden brown and done (to test, insert knife in center — when it comes out clean bread is done). Makes 2 large or 3 medium loaves.

## *Another recipe for fasting bread*

*For 2lb. of flour, add in the following order:*

*25 ½ oz. lukewarm water (about 98° F)*

*1tsp sugar*

*1tsp baker's yeast*

*Mix well, and then add:*

*2 tbs. oil; 1tbs. salt, 1 ½ cup rolled oats (oat meal)*

Preparation:

Mix all ingredients. Add small amounts of flour as needed, if dough is too thin.

Let stand 2 hours minimum (or all night) in a warm, even temperature location (not under 77° F) covered with a damp cloth.

Place the dough (about 1 ½ inch thick) in a well-oiled baking pan.

Let stand for 30 minutes.

Place in oven pre-heated at 320° and cook 50 to 60 min.

The quality of the bread will vary mostly according to the type of flour used. Whole wheat and white flours may be mixed.

*Our Bread Maker Machine, one of the many available on the market*

## Spelt Bread

*2 lbs whole meal spelt flour*

*1 lb wheat flour*

*2 teaspoons salt*

*1 ½ pkgs. baking yeast*

*3.5 oz milk*

*1 teaspoon sugar*

*½ cup of warm water*

*1 handful peeled sunflower seeds*

Mix flour, salt and sunflower seeds in a kneading bowl. Dissolve sugar in warmed milk, add crumbled yeast and stir. Make a well in the flour mixture, put in the yeast solution and cover with some flour, leave 15 minutes for fermentation. Add enough warm water to give a dough which can be well kneaded. Knead vigorously until the dough is detaching from the bowl. Leave to rest ½ to ¾ of an hour. Knead dough on floured surface. Shape into six loafs, put on a greased baking tin. Let rise for another ½ hour. Bake in oven for about 45 minutes. One loaf is just right for two people; the rest is kept in the freezer.

This basic formula can be varied in different mode: spelt and wheat flour can be mixed in all proportions; pure whole meal spelt bread is very good. Spelt adapts well to recipes recommending more conventional flour; just use a little more spelt flour and a little less liquid. Spelt bread is less liable to crumble and dry out. It remains juicier and has more aromatic taste. Wheat and rye grits, rolled oats, oilseeds or spices can be added. When you use rye flour, some acidifying agent should be added: sourdough, sour milk products or the like.

*Indian flat bread* is also good: prepare dough from 1 lb whole meal spelt flour and 1 lb wheat flour, spread on a baking tin, cover stripes with rolled oats, caraway, poppy, and sesame, sunflower or pumpkin seeds.

*Whole-grain spelt kernels:* rinse and soak 8-12 hours before cooking (optional, to release nutrients and make any grain more digestible). Use 3 cups water for every 1 cup spelt (will almost triple). Place spelt and water in a pot and bring to the boil. Reduce to a simmer, cover, and cook 2 hours, until the kernels are soft and all water is absorbed. They can be cooked as a quick porridge or added to homemade muesli and bread mixes. Green spelt is harvested before it is ripe, has no flavor and can be bad for health.

## *Marie-Line's recipe*

*For 1 ½ lbs (650 gr) of whole spelt flour*

*1. In a small bowl, place 1 tsp. (5 ml) of dry yeast in 5 ½ tblsp (80 ml) of water at 98.6°F (37° C). Add 1 tsp. (5 ml) of sugar. Let it stand for 10 min or until the volume doubles.*

*2. Put 1 ½ c. (350 ml) of warm water in a large bowl.*

*3. Add 1 ½ teaspoons of salt and 4 tsps (20 ml) of coconut or olive oil. Mix.*

*4. Gradually add the flour while kneading.*

*5. Cover with a damp cloth and let it rise for 60 min in a warm place at 77-86°F (25°-30° C.)*

*6. Remove the cloth, punch down the dough and let stand 30 more minutes covered with the damp cloth. Let it rise again in a warm place, at around 82° F. (28° C.)*

*7. Grease a loaf pan.*

*8. Remove the cloth and shape a loaf of bread using a little flour on a flat surface.*

*9. Leave to rise for about 20 minutes in a warm place.*

*10. Bake in the center of the oven at 350° F (175° C) for 50 minutes.*

Many people make the mistake of putting the dough into the oven at low temperatures in order to let it rise better. However, the oven is too hot and the bread falls. The dough must rise slowly, at room temperature. Putting it into the oven to rise with just the light on is the right technique.

Note: There are low-cost bread machines that will allow you to make bread in two or three hours depending on the appliance. Just put in the ingredients and the bread will come out ready to be eaten. This allows those who are fasting to choose their flour and have real "home-made" bread without spending too much time on it. (This is also a good gift idea for your friends! )

## *Sister Sarah's recipe for fasting bread*

*For 10 cups (1k or 2.2 lbs) of cereal flour 3tbs instant baker's yeast*

*1.5 tsp salt*

*2 tbs oil (olive, sunflower or other)*

Knead flour with yeast, salt and oil.

Add a little warm water at a time until the dough comes off the hands.

Let rise near source of heat.

Put into bread pans (3 pans for 1k). Let dough rise longer.

Bake in oven at 375º F (190ºC or gas mark 5) 25 to 30min

Watch!

## *Flavia's Recipe for Fasting bread Made without yeast like chapattis in India*

*Ingredients for about 6 servings: 2 ½ cups of whole wheat flour*

*¾ cup of white flour*

*½ tsp salt*

*2 ½ tbs olive oil 1 ½ cup of water*

*¼ - ½ cup of ground almonds (or other nut); optional 1/3 cup of raisins soaked in a cup of very hot water; optional.*

## *Instructions*

Soak the raisins in a cup of very hot water to become plumb, about 15 min.

Preheat oven to 400 degrees F (or 200 degrees C). Then combine all ingredients in a bowl. The mixture should be very wet.

Add mixture to a non-stick pan or grease a glass baking dish.

With hands or spoon, pat and smooth the mixture evenly on the bottom of the pan. Bake for 15 min on the top rack, then remove and place on the bottom rack for another 15 min.

When firm to the touch, and the sides are crispy and pulling away from the pan, it is done. Leave to cool slightly. Remove from pan and serve immediately.

## *Gluten-Free Fasting Bread Recipe*

*From a bakery, in Italy*

*Makes approximately 1 ¾ lbs (800g) of bread*

*1 cup (250 g) light brown rice flour*

*½ c. (100 g) chestnut flour*

*½ c. (100 g) corn flour*

*¼ c. (50 g) potato starch*

*1 ounce (20 g) fresh Baker's yeast or ¼ ounce (7 g) dry yeast*

*1 ½ ounce (50 g) honey*

*1 ¼ c. (300ml) warm water 2 tbs olive oil*

*1 pinch fine salt*

Mix your different types of flour and the salt. Mix water, yeast, honey and oil.

Add your liquid mix to the flour. Mix and stir vigorously with a wooden spoon!

Leave to rise for one hour in the bowl, then place the dough in a loaf pan.

Leave to rise at room temperature for 50 min.

Bake in a hot oven 410°F (210°C) for 25 minutes, then lower the temperature and continue baking for 20 min!

## *For a bread loaf of about 1.5 pounds (with dry fruits) in the bread machine. On cycle for wheat:*

> 1 1/2 cup of whole grain flour; 2 cups of white flour;
>
> 1 1/2 teaspoon of instant dry yeast; 1 1/2 teaspoons of salt;
>
> 1/4 cup of raisins (any other dry fruit); 1/4 cup of almonds;
>
> 1/4 cup of sunflower seeds; 2 tablespoons of muesli;
>
> 1 1/2 cup of warm water;
>
> 1/4 cup olive oil (or another oil).

Place dry yeast, flour, salt, raisins, almonds, sunflower seeds, muesli, water, and olive oil in bread pan. Turn on and set bread machine. Add water if dough does not come together or white flour if dough sticks to sides of pan.

*For a bread loaf of about 1lb (without dry fruits) in the bread machine. On cycle for Wheat or Integral:*

> 1 1/4 cups warm water; 1/2 teaspoon salt;
>
> 1 1/2 cups whole grain flour; 2 cups white bread flour;
>
> 3 tablespoons olive oil;
>
> 1 1/2 teaspoons active dry yeast; 1 cup warm water.

Place dry yeast, flour, salt, water, and olive oil in bread pan. Turn on and set bread machine. Add water if dough does not come together or white flour if dough sticks to the sides of the pan.

*Recipe for flat rye loaves*

> 2.2lb white flour 2.2lb whole rye flour 1tbs vegetable oil
>
> 4 ½ cup water
>
> A pinch of baking powder; a pinch of salt 1tsp sugar
>
> 1 packet (about 1/3 oz.) yeast

Preparation:

Mix yeast, one tbs. of flour and one tsp. of sugar together, and then add it to two cups of warm water to let the yeast rise.

Mix the other ingredients together and add the yeast and the rest of the water. Knead until you can form a compact and smooth ball.

Divide into 20 to 25 pieces and roll them into balls. Cover them with a damp cloth and place in the refrigerator. Will keep two to three days.

To cook, spread the dough into miniature pizza crusts. Bake in the oven at maximum temperature.

Serve the breads as soon as they are cooked; they lose flavor and texture as they cool.

## *Recipe for English bread*

*9 oz. white wheat flour and 9 oz. whole wheat flour*

*1 ½ tsp salt*

*1oz. fresh yeast*

*2 oz. butter*

*1 cup water*

*1 tsp lemon juice*

Preparation:

Mix flour, salt, water, lemon juice. Add butter, and then yeast.

Let rise 60 to 90 minutes.

Fold dough 4 or 5 times and squeeze it with your hands while digging in underneath to let air in.

Form into a ball slightly flattened on the top. Let rise another 30 to 45 minutes depending on ambient temperature.

Pre-heat oven to 430° F.

Brush surface with milk or one beaten egg, sprinkle with flour, and make cuts in the surface, widening each cut towards the end.

Place on a sheet of parchment paper and cook 20 to 30 minutes, depending on the oven.

The bread is done when it sounds hollow.

# Other Books from the Author

*The Forgotten Power of Fasting*
*healing, liberation, joy …*

"I read your book from cover to cover. Your words completely captivated me and have convinced me on the importance of fasting. I knew already the benefits of fasting, but I wasn't aware of all its attributes, that you explain so well. Reading this book one discovers fasting.

As we know, Our Lady in Medjugorje continuously insists on the importance of fasting, but we avoid putting into practice something when it means we have to make a sacrifice. We struggle to convince ourselves to actually fast.

The arguments you present, and the examples that you give in this book, show very clearly the reason why Our Lady insists so persistently on something so precious for the soul and the body, for the apostolate on earth and for the souls in Purgatory. I thank you for emphasizing such an important topic, very often mentioned in Sacred Scripture, so precious for the living and for the intercession of the dead.

The final part of your work, with the words from the saints, will convince even the most reluctant.

This book will be nothing less than a true discovery of fasting to whoever reads it."

*Don Gabriele Amorth*

Euro 7.00
Sister Emmanuel
© 1995 Children of Medjugorje
www.sremmanuel.org

*Children, Help My Heart To Triumph!*

At the height of the Bosnian War, Sister Emmanuel remained in Medjugorje with a few members of her community. During that time, memories of her father, a Prisoner of War during WWII, continually surfaced. Remembering how much he suffered, she felt a need to do something to spiritually help those on the front lines. Sister Emmanuel describes a call that she received at that time to appeal to the children for their sacrifices in order to alleviate the war. *Children, Help My Heart To Triumph* was written in response to that call. It describes for children how to make a 9-day novena of little sacrifices. Included is a coloring book that they can color and mail to Medjugorje where they will be presented at one of Our Lady's apparitions.

US $ 11.99<br>
Sister Emmanuel<br>
© 1996 Children of Medjugorje<br>
Reprinted 2012 Includes Coloring Book<br>
www.sremmanuel.org

*The Amazing Secret of the Souls in Purgatory*

It is not often that a book touches the soul so deeply. *The Amazing Secret of the Souls in Purgatory* is such a book. Maria Simma, deceased in March of 2003, lived a humble life in the mountains of Austria. When she was twenty-five, Maria was graced with a very special charism—the charism of being visited by the many souls in Purgatory—and being able to communicate with them! Maria shares, in her own words, some amazing secrets about the souls in Purgatory. She answers questions such as: What is Purgatory? How do souls get there? Who decides if a soul goes to Purgatory? How can we help get souls released from Purgatory?

US $ 8.99
© 1997 Queenship Publishing
www.queenship.org
www.sremmanuel.org

*The Hidden Child of Medjugorje*

"Reading "Medjugorje, the 90s" had left me dazzled and so deeply touched that it had literally pulled me to Medjugorje. I just had to see with my own eyes the spiritual wonders retold in that book. Now with "The Hidden Child," the ember of love for Mary has received a new breath of air—a Pentecostal wind. Sr. Emmanuel is indeed one of Mary's best voices! Congratulations for this jewel of a testimonial! I wouldn't be surprised if the Gospa herself turned out to be Sister's most avid reader."

*Msgr. Denis Croteau, OMI*

"Books are like seashells; at first they all look alike. However, they are far from being identical and their value varies greatly. Some of them are packed with riches and so well written, that they hide rare pearls within. Sister Emmanuel's book is one of those; it contains the most beautiful pearls, and with them enriches the reader. Through her accounts and anecdotes, the reader is pleased to meet people of great worth and to be filled with the teachings of so many events. Through this book, one will explore more fully a way still too little known: the way of the Queen of Peace."

*Fr. Jozo Zovko, OFM*

US $ 15.99
Sister Emmanuel
© 2010 Children of Medjugorje, Inc.
www.sremmanuel.org

*Maryam of Bethlehem, the Little Arab*

Who is this little Arab? Maryam Baouardy is a daughter of Galilee. Her life? A succession of supernatural manifestations worthy of Catherine of Sienna. Maryam shares the keys of holiness, including ways to defeat Satan himself. This is a book you don't want to miss?

US $ 5.00<br>
Sister Emmanuel<br>
© 2012 Children of Medjugorje, Inc.<br>
www.sremmanuel.org<br>
*Available in E-Book*

*The Beautiful Story of Medjugorje
As Told to Children from 7 to 97*

In this book, you will follow the experiences of six little shepherds, their shock when they saw the "Lady" appearing to them in 1981. You will see how Vicka and Jokov actually experienced the reality of life beyond this world, when Our Lady took them with her on the most extraordinary journey to Heaven, Purgatory and Hell.

You will learn how brave they were under persecution. You will be excited to know the mes—sages they share from a Mother who thinks only of helping us, who loves each one of us so much—including you in a very special way!

You will read about the powerful healings of bodies and souls happening there, as in Lourdes.

This is an adventure story, except that this story is true and is happening right now for you!

US $ 5.00
Sister Emmanuel
© 2012 Children of Medjugorje
www.sremmanuel.org
*Available in E-Book*

*Peace will have the last word*

The mercy of God is scandalous, it even borders on the extreme! In her engaging and lively style, Sister Emmanuel recounts real life stories and testimonies that take the reader's heart on a journey of God's mercy, passing through the prisons of New York, and into the confessionals of the Saints!

In these pages, a mosaic of photos and parables, the reader encounters the very depths of the human heart and is transported into the midst of scenes and situations that are as captivating as they are diverse. Through them we witness that much-desired peace that comes from Above, gaining victory over emptiness, futility and fear.

Here are words that many no longer dare to speak, and yet, they have the power to help rebuild a degenerating society. This book is a shot in the arm, an injection of hope that will hasten the time when, in the hearts of all, peace will have the last word!

US $ 13.99
Sister Emmanuel
© 2015 Children of Medjugorje
www.sremmanuel.org

*Scandalous Mercy*
*when god goes beyond the boundaries*

Why Scandalous Mercy?

In these pages the reader will discover unexplored aspects of the Heart of God that you might think are crazy! Crazy with love! You will meet Mother Teresa, Maryam of Bethlehem, a Nazi criminal, a priest condemned to hell, a high ranking abortionist, a drug dealer from Brazil, a furious mother-in-law, a sick child…and in the middle of all this, the most beautiful Heart of Christ, who is calling ALL His children.

This beautiful selection of testimonies and "little flowers" picked from everyday life will capture the reader on two levels: first, the reader of this book will find his achy heart soothed and enriched by new ways to find hope in our difficult world today; second, he will be shocked to learn that these stories are true. They will make you laugh, cry, even tremble, but one thing is certain, they will all amaze you!

US $ 13.00
Sister Emmanuel
© 2015 Children of Medjugorje
www.sremmanuel.org

*Medjugorje, Triumph of the Heart*
*revised edition of medjugorje of the 90s*

Sister Emmanuel offers a pure echo of Medjugorje, the eventful village where the Mother of God has been appearing since 1981. She shares at length some of the personal stories of the villagers, the visionaries, and the pilgrims who flock there by the thousands, receiving great healings. Eight years of awe have inspired this book. these 89 stories offer a glimpse into the miracles of Mary's motherly love.

US $ 12.95
Sister Emmanuel
© 2015 Children of Medjugorje
www.sremmanuel.org

# About the Author

Sister Emmanuel Maillard was born in France in 1947. After completing a degree in Literature and History of Fine Arts at the Sorbonne University in Paris, she studied theology with Cardinal Daniélou. In 1973, she had a powerful experience of the love of Jesus and she decided to consecrate her life to God. In 1976 she joined the Community of the Beatitudes in France, which she is still part of. In 1989, she received a call from the Blessed Mother and she was sent by her community to Medjugorje where she still lives. Since 1992 and from there she has been travelling around the world to evangelize and bring hope to a society that often looks for happiness where it gets lost.

Her books have been translated into several languages and have touched the hearts of many readers around the world, quickly becoming best-sellers. Her talks and testimonies have also been publicized through CDs, TV shows, internet and other media.

One can find the list of her works on www.chidrenofmedjugorje.com in order to receive her monthly newsletter, please register at:

commentscom@childrenofmedjugorje.com

www.ingramcontent.com/pod-product-compliance
Lightning Source LLC
Chambersburg PA
CBHW070428010526
44118CB00014B/1947